THE
CHURCH
HAS LEFT THE
BUILDING

THE
CHURCH
HAS LEFT THE
BUILDING

AN APPEAL FOR CHURCH LEADERS TO GET BACK TO THE BASICS

JIM HAYFORD

WinePressPublishing
Great Books, Defined.

WinePress Publishing (PO Box 428, Enumclaw, WA 98022) functions only as book publisher. As such, the ultimate design, content, editorial accuracy, and views expressed or implied in this work are those of the author.

The author of this book has waived a portion of the publisher's recommended professional editing services. As such, any related errors found in this finished product are not the responsibility of the publisher.

Unless otherwise noted, all Scriptures are taken from the *Holy Bible, New International Version®, NIV®*. Copyright © 1973, 1978, 1984 by Biblica, Inc.™ Used by permission of Zondervan. All rights reserved worldwide. www.zondervan.com

Scripture references marked KJV are taken from the *King James Version* of the Bible.

Scripture references marked NASB are taken from the *New American Standard Bible,* © 1960, 1963, 1968, 1971, 1972, 1973, 1975, 1977 by The Lockman Foundation. Used by permission.

ISBN 13: 978-1-4141-2086-7
ISBN 10: 1-4141-2086-9
Library of Congress Catalog Card Number: 2011927074

DEDICATED TO

My wife, Betsey, who has encouraged and joined me through the long search for authentic Christianity.

My children, Laurie, Jim Jr., and Steve, who were there all the time, deeply caring about what their mom and dad were trying to do.

My mentors, Don McGregor and Jerry Cook, who helped me believe that there were others who were earnestly seeking a church like the church we read about in *The Acts of the Apostles*.

My dear friends, Harold & Loretta Huston, who have believed in me and supported my dreams and visions over the years.

CONTENTS

PREFACE

I T SEEMS TO me that it is about time for the church to come to grips with the fact that we barely resemble today the church we read about in the book of Acts. We have spent the last 2,000 years complicating and codifying Christianity. In our sincere, yet often misguided, efforts to "spruce up" the church, perhaps we have only further confused an on-looking world that is searching for God; yet puzzled them with the games we, His church, are so often playing.

This book is from my heart as I have pursued a personal quest for authentic church life that kept taking me back to the Bible. There I found something not so institutionally defined as with the church I grew up knowing. There I found a community of believers who were not as predictable as the tidy traditions and structures that surround the name of Jesus today. There I discovered that to recover the dynamic and the simplicity of the early church, it would require a stance that I call: "Contending for the Authentic." There I discovered a church not defined by its architecture.

You are invited to read this book and take a trip to the New Testament, where early believers had not yet had sufficient time to clutter their faith with robes and jewels. Church life was practical, personal, and powerful. This author believes that that model of church life is still applicable today and can be applied by anyone who wants it with all of their heart.

FOREWORD

A WELL-KNOWN MISSIONARY WROTE a summary of leaders he saw as being significant instruments influencing the present work of God around the world. Among several dozen names he mentioned two—my brother, Jim, and me.

I was gratified for one essential reason. It wasn't for the honor of being included in his list at all, nor was it because of the writer's overly generous comparison made of "the Hayford brothers" in the 20th century and "the Wesley brothers" in the 18th, as men influencing renewal in the church. But I was moved because the writer joined my name to my brother's – a fact which caused me to rejoice because of the respect I have for Jim.

There are few people I have met like him, who can so skillfully and practically set forth the vital essence of the New Testament church's real vision. You can see what I mean here. There is a clarity and conciseness in these pages – timely, terse statements – which anyone can understand without confusion and can apply without complication.

Reading *The Church Has Left the Building* has served as a renewed summons to my own soul. Inherent in these pages is more than a plan – this is the stuff of spiritual awakening! Priorities are focused and possibilities are unfolded, and in the midst of it power begins to flow. You can feel the Holy Spirit breathing here because at the heart of each proposition is the Word of God.

But there is also a very pragmatic reason for pursuing the contents of this book: *it's been tested!* Not only has the author applied these principles with great fruitfulness at two different pastorates, but also the core of these concepts provides the working foundation for thousands of living, growing congregations around the world.

In hundreds of those cases, the spark that ignited the local leader was the author himself. Jim's pastoral ministry has been extended to encourage and help shape the thinking of many leaders through his participation in national and international leadership seminars. More and more men and women in church ministry are learning that this man "has the goods." Jim brings something of the spiritual reality and practical vitality available for personal and corporate application by perceptive leaders.

So you can see why I'm so pleased to introduce these pages to you and why I felt so honored Jim asked me to do so. As you begin reading and processing your way through this wealth of workable insights, you'll also see why I am justifiably proud to be known as Jim Hayford's brother.

—Dr. Jack W. Hayford
The Kings University
Van Nuys, California

INTRODUCTION

I FIRST WROTE PORTIONS of this book twenty years ago as a summary from my experience of growth and ministry in the San Francisco Bay Area in a church-planting situation that blossomed into a church of 2,000 members. It was a self-published work read by a few thousand people. Some told me it changed their way of thinking about ministry. I recently picked up a fading copy of it to review, and when I laid it down I thought to myself, "This book was written before its time." So I have edited it, given it a new title, and offer it to you – maybe for the first time or possibly the second.

In the past twenty years, the American Church has continued to languish except for some emerging "hot spots" – usually mega-churches that are more the exception than the rule. Organized Christianity continues to market the Christian faith as some kind of a commodity rather than a way of life. My heart has always been for the guy/gal out there faithfully pastoring the people of God, but most of the time feeling forgotten and frustrated or even depressed about the inertia that seems to characterize the congregations they lead. Inevitably, the question that comes to mind is, "What's wrong with me?" This question is a self-defeating "rabbit hole" that seldom leads to any sort of positive transformation, personally or corporately. What's wrong? What needs to get fixed? In my humble opinion it is the basic way we "do" church that needs our attention. Most of us are frustrated because we have been sold an *attractional* style of Christianity rather than an *incarnational* approach that values servanthood not celebrity, relationship not program, and sacrifice not greed.

The Church Has Left the Building harkens back to a time when the church had no facilities, no programs, and was slightly disorganized! The emphasis was people...period. My simple definition of "the church" is: anyone washed in the blood of Jesus Christ. Jesus did not die for real estate, liturgies, bylaws, or worship styles. This book, partially written twenty years ago, is even more timely today than it was back then!

STARTING FROM SCRATCH

This story begins way back in 1977. Encouraged by friends and helped by our denomination, we settled in Danville, California, knowing absolutely no one at all. The night we arrived, after bidding farewell to our loving and well-wishing congregation in Glendale four hundred miles to the south, found us sleeping on the floor of a rented house, surrounded by a slumbering community that had no idea that we had arrived, and frankly couldn't have cared less.

There we were, a family of five, filled with expectations, dreams, and certainly fears as we faced the awesome task of planting a New Testament church "from scratch." We had never done anything like that before, but we knew beyond the shadow of a doubt that God was in it with us, so we set to work in Jesus' name. Little could we have imagined what the Lord would do in raising up a vibrant and significant New Testament church that still flourishes today!

THE FOUNDING VISION

"Announcing," the simple newspaper article declared, *"a family-centered, Bible-believing, charismatic church...."* One month after arriving in town we were ready to conduct our first public meeting. We rented the multi-purpose room of an elementary school and notified anyone who would read the local paper that Zion Fellowship of Danville* was "open for business."

In the Sundays, months, and years to follow that fall day in 1977, a church was born and began to thrive in the green valley of San Ramon, thirty miles east of the Golden Gate. In the twelve years we served there the congregation grew to some 1,500 members and their children, sponsored the birth or rebirth of thirteen other congregations, operated a Ministry Institute that prepared scores for full-time ministry, and erected a 55,000 square foot "Gathering Place" on a seven-acre plot of land strategically set in the middle of the cluster of towns and cities the church served.

Habakkuk 2:2 says: *"Write down the revelation and make it plain on tablets so that a herald may run with it."* Early into the founding of the church, the following "Founding Vision" was published:

> "To establish in the San Francisco-Oakland Bay Area a church that would be as much like the New Testament as possible, for we believe that it is those kind of people for which the Lord is returning. This fellowship of believers would be interdenominational in spirit and image. The ministry would grow to include: a system of fellowship

groups meeting in scores of homes; a training center for men and women who desire to plant similar churches in the Bay Area of Northern California and the mission field; a Christian school; an aggressive outreach to youth; active involvement in spiritual warfare, intercession and unity emphasis for the Bay Area's much needed revival. Above all, the vision is to see a strong, viable, family-centered charismatic church thriving in the San Ramon Valley."

With the exception of the Christian school, this vision was realized to a degree greater than our wildest imaginations. Incidentally, the only reason we did not start a school was because another church in the Valley was committed to that vision, and seeing they had the "grace" to do it well, we saw no need in being redundant.

This book was written, and recently rewritten, to summarize and present the philosophy of ministry that evolved from this church-plant, and has become my "modus-operandi" in pastorates over subsequent years. Now, as I am retiring from senior pastoring, I give these principles to the next generation of church leaders for their careful and prayerful consideration.

*Today the church is called East Bay Fellowship.

SEEING VISIONS…DREAMING DREAMS

"In the last days," God says, *"I will pour out my spirit on all people. Your sons and daughters will prophesy, your young men will see visions, your old men will dream dreams."*

In the summer of 1965, Martin Luther King stood on the steps of the Capitol Building in Washington D.C. He delivered a speech to the throng assembled there that day that has become the standard-bearer for the Civil Rights movement ever since, and what most would call a "classic" expression of the human heart. Of course, I am referring to his famous "I Have a Dream" sermon. That day he was able to identify and effectively communicate his very reason for living. As he poured out his heart, he was actually giving to his listeners his definition of why he existed – it was his very life message reduced to a collection of words.

When an individual is able to articulate what is in their heart, they are able to find focus and gain momentum toward the very accomplishment for which before they could only ponder, wonder, and hope.

Some time back, Law Professor Sanford Levinson of Yale University made a thorough study regarding the effect that aspirations, plans, and convictions (or "dreams") have on human behavior. Here are a few of his findings:

1. The earliest dreams of young people are usually ill-defined, outlandishly inflated, and often too sizeable to reach.
2. Later in adult life the dream is formulated, more practical, and measurable.
3. People, who for various reasons never really formulate a dream, tend to live lives of general disorder. They drift from job to job and struggle with their self worth.

THERE MUST BE MORE

The passage of Scripture quoted by Peter from the writings of the prophet Joel that constituted his Day of Pentecost sermon, took on new meaning for me one day as I wrestled with my frustration and concern about being a pastor and the general condition of the church of Jesus Christ. I knew that good things were happening, but I also realized we were barely "scraping the surface," so to speak, of addressing the true needs of the people. I looked around. Sure there were success stories, and in every direction I looked, pastors and people were busy for God. But I kept asking myself, "What's really going on in these people's lives? Do we know…can we know? Maybe we really don't want to know - I just don't know."

As a young pastor, I determined to find out as much as I could about how the church could actually and measurably identify and meet people's needs in the power of the Holy Spirit. Frankly, after so many years of attending church and now pastoring a church, my wife and I agreed that we were both tired of "playing church." In fact, we realized that if we did not find some of these answers, we would soon become a statistic; two more of the thousands of "called ones" who depart the ministry in search of "greener pastures."

Like Professor Levinson found in his studies, we had goals – exciting, ambitious plans that had propelled us to that point in serving God. Most of them had been realized. However, like the plea of the rich young man who came to Jesus in Matthew 19:20, we still cried out to the Lord saying, *"What do we still lack?"*

BACK TO THE BIBLE

The Lord gave us the sense to know that the answers to our questions and the end of our frustrations did not lie in a new program or another seminar. He sent us from our knees back to the Bible.

At that particular time, in addition to pastoring our small church, I was serving as an adjunct member of the faculty of a nearby Bible college. The course of study assigned to me in the upcoming semester was entitled "The Acts and Life of Paul." With that discipline ahead of me, I purposed in my heart that another look at the Acts of the

Apostles was to be for me more than just preparation of lectures to be presented to a class of college sophomores. It would be a personal odyssey, led by the Spirit of God, that would bring me to a definition of "church" and "ministry" that would preserve my wife and myself for pastoral service and bring us finally to never having to "play church" again. I might add, I have continued to read and reread the Acts of the Apostles over the years as my personal "Guidebook to Pastoring."

THE DREAM

I discovered that the early dreams, mostly quantitative, that I had when we began public ministry no longer sufficed. In fact, they had driven me for years. They had pushed and prodded me to what some considered very high levels of achievement within my denomination and peer group. The "flip side" of that, however, was the subtle crowding out of other important priorities in order to accomplish the "dream." Family, personal health, and spiritual formation all suffered in the mad dash to achieve the goals.

I felt sorry for the "dreamless people" I had met along the way, and purposed in my heart that I would never be like that. But at some point, the early dream ran out of gas. It didn't satisfy anymore. Ministry had to mean more than just keeping the "ecclesiastical machine" rolling along. I met some ministers along the way who never had a dream and were content not to think about it very much. They lived for today, taking little thought for the future. In some respects that philosophy almost sounded biblical. Didn't Jesus say something like that? (They seemed to forget that the context of that admonition in Matthew 6 has to do with worrying, not planning.)

The book of Acts read like an adventure novel as I searched its pages in a quest for a dream. I didn't know at the time that I was desperately looking for something for which to live...and then, there it was! Coming out of the pages was a church, a community of believers who were having a viable impact upon their towns and cities. They loved, they ministered, they failed, they cared, they laughed and they cried – together. That was what we were looking for, and it was there all of the time!

THE DREAM:

That There Could Be Today a Church Like the Church We Read About in Acts!

That's it. Not particularly profound and not anything new. (A lot of people have that dream.) But now it was ours, and we were ready to follow it into the rest of our lives with the Bible as our guide and the Lord Jesus as our strength!

. . . .

CHAPTER 1

THE JERUSALEM CHURCH REVISITED

"They devoted themselves to the apostles' teaching and to fellowship, to the breaking of bread and prayer. Everyone was filled with awe, and many wonders and miraculous signs were done by the apostles.

"All the believers were together and had everything in common. Selling their possessions and goods, they gave to anyone as he had need. Every day they continued to meet together in the temple courts. They broke bread in their homes, and ate together with glad and sincere hearts, praising God and enjoying the favor of all the people. And the Lord added to their number daily those who were being saved."

—Acts 2:42-47 (NIV)

THE SECOND CHAPTER of Acts gives us the extraordinary account of the birth of the church – *"When the Day of Pentecost came...."* Today we speed through the text, thrilled by the events of this day like no other day. The small but faithful group of Jesus' followers was

1

sequestered in a safe place somewhere in Jerusalem, waiting for something they didn't understand – a counselor, a Paraclete. Nevertheless, they were waiting because Jesus had promised. He had always kept His word, so they waited. You know the story – a rushing wind, tongues of fire and suddenly common people speaking languages they were incapable of learning. As they declared the wonders of God in their newfound tongues, passersby overhearing the praise gathered and questioned with curiosity the sincerity of "Galileans," (an unlearned lot) who were boldly and fluently worshipping God in their native languages.

How many times have we read and reread Peter's powerful sermon? This once wincing and cowardly man now, by the Spirit's strength, courageously preached to the gathering crowd his explanation of what was going on. His unabashed testimony that *"Jesus, whom you crucified [is] both Lord and Christ"* along with his passionate invitation for those listening to *"receive the gift of the Holy Spirit"* results in the rest of the day being spent baptizing the approximately 3,000 people who received the message in faith, embracing Jesus of Nazareth as their Messiah.

Yes, we all know that story. It "preaches well," and all of God's children read the account of the birth of the church with satisfaction. In fact, sometimes we fail to read the rest of the chapter, as though we were somehow exhausted from experiencing the blessing of the first forty-one verses of this epoch chapter.

But quietly, persistently creeping out from under the glory cloud of the Day of Pentecost emerges a paragraph of verses that demand of us the same kind of attention and reverence we have given to those that precede it. A "peek," if you will, a virtual glimpse at what life was like in the community that developed among the believers there in Jerusalem in the days, months, and years immediately following the Day of Pentecost.

THEY DEVOTED THEMSELVES

They earnestly persevered, or "continued steadfast" as the King James Version puts it. These words embody a value that is quickly losing ground in our time. The idea that "devotion to duty" would be appropriate to one's "religious practices" today seems out of place, or perhaps a bit fanatical. After all, it would seem one could have a personal conviction about the things of God without getting too "carried away" with a lot of passion, don't you think?

The people we read about in the last six verses of Acts 2 were not "playing church." The qualities listed here were more than role-playing or a hollow routine learned through generations of church attendance.

This was the beginning – the precedent. They were on the cutting edge. No examples existed, save what they had picked up from Jesus personally (remember they were "eyewitnesses") and the traditions of their Jewish fathers and mothers. It would not be easy for them, but, as He had done in the past before He left them, Jesus would show them that new and better way.

The ancient Chinese proverb, "The beginning of a thousand-mile journey is one step," certainly applies here. The destination of the early believers' walk was inestimable. They would only follow Jesus one step at a time.

Verse 47 clearly shows us that the Lord knew where they were heading. This verse teaches us that if we will do our part, He will do His. **Our part:** follow Him carefully, devotedly, one step at a time. **His part:** *"and the Lord added to their number daily those who were being saved."* He will build His church. He will care for His own and He will bring them to their destination. All the while, He will be providing His people with the thrill of personal and corporate growth and blessing.

OUR PART

These six incredible verses include at least a dozen characteristics of church life. There is hidden in this passage a veritable gold mine of spiritual and relational dynamics that the Holy Spirit made possible in and through the lives of the early believers in Jerusalem. While we know that this fledgling group of believers was not by any stretch of the imagination perfect, they were, however, the genuine article. The behavior that developed among them was uncluttered, very simple and designed to deal directly with the practical challenges of everyday life. Sensitively, these people cared about each other deeply. Empowered by the Spirit of God, they reached out to each other with hospitality and compassion. They were very sane about the whole thing. While miraculous occurrences seemed to be almost commonplace with them, they had a reverent spirit; and even those who watched from a safe distance of unbelief respected them for their sincerity.

They were sound, solidly based in Scripture, which they regularly heard read at the Temple and from the apostles who carefully passed on to them the teachings of Jesus. The early believers were on to something. It was born in the heart of Jesus Himself when He had said: *"I will build my church and the gates of Hell will not prevail against it"* (Matthew 16:18). It was enabled when they obeyed His parting command to *"stay in the city until you have been clothed with power from on high"* (Luke 24:49).

There are some very important lessons for each of us to learn from these people. With single-minded purpose and

4

steadfastness they served the Lord and each other simply, sensitively, sanely, and soundly. They did their part – and He did His.

A CLOSER LOOK

The twelve characteristics of church life found in Acts 2:42 deserve a closer look. While this book in no way attempts to be a technical commentary on the book of Acts, there is more for us to know about this passage than just what "meets the eye."

CHARACTERISTIC	PRACTICAL DEFINITION
1. "Apostles' teaching"	The love and obedience to God's Word

Ministry Principle: A New Testament church believes and teaches that the Holy Bible is God's Word. It holds to the plenary verbal inspiration of the Scriptures. It encourages God's people to find the standard for all of their life in the Word of God. (2 Timothy 3:16)

2. "Fellowship"	The pleasure like-minded people find in each other's company.

Ministry Principle: A New Testament church believes and teaches that God's people need each other. It holds to the conviction that ministry flows through relationships. It encourages people to develop meaningful, familial and accountable relationships. (Hebrews 10:25)

3. **"Breaking of bread"**   The sharing of our salvation through Jesus Christ in the remembrance of His sacrifice.

Ministry Principle: A New Testament church believes and teaches the centrality of the cross of Jesus Christ. It holds to mankind's need for personal salvation through Jesus Christ. It encourages God's people to obey the Lord Jesus in remembering His death until He comes through observing the Lord's table. (1 Corinthians 11:26)

4. **"Prayer"**   The acknowledgment of our mutual need for communication with God.

Ministry Principle: A New Testament church believes and teaches that prayer is an indispensable part of a person's relationship with God. It holds to the conviction that God hears the prayer of faith. It encourages God's people to grow and mature in "all kinds of prayer." (Philippians 4:6)

5. **"Filled with awe"**   The appropriate response to the living presence of God.

Ministry Principle: A New Testament church believes and teaches that God's presence is to be expected and sought. It holds to the biblical example of reverence and respect for the things of God. It encourages God's people to cultivate sensitivity to the will and ways of God. (1 Corinthians 14:40)

6. **"Wonders and miraculous signs"**   The grace of God on display in the midst of His people.

Ministry Principle: A New Testament church believes and teaches that God's supernatural power is real and available today. It holds to the conviction that signs and wonders are not to be considered a curiosity, but a reality. It encourages God's people to make themselves available to be ministers of the gifts of the Holy Spirit. (1 Peter 3:10)

7. "Were together"   The interdependent nature of God's people through love.

Ministry Principle: A New Testament church believes and teaches that love characterized by unconditional acceptance of one another is the release point of the Holy Spirit's work. It holds to the priority of compassion and openness in giving testimony of Jesus Christ. It encourages God's people to mature in trustworthiness and dependability towards one another. (John 13:34, 35)

8. "Had everything   The unselfish nature of Jesus at
   in common"   work in practical ways.

Ministry Principle: A New Testament church believes and teaches that all God's people possess in actuality is the Lord's. It holds to a mentality of focusing on people's needs, and meeting them in God's strength. It encourages God's people to be sensitive to each other's needs, and to ask the Lord to show them how they can be an answer to people's prayers. (Acts 4:34)

9. "Met together in   The celebration and instruc-
   the temple courts"   tion made possible when
                        "God's people" all get together.

Ministry Principle: A New Testament church believes and teaches the fundamental importance of the assembling together of God's people. It holds to the fact that spiritual maturity and blessing were designed by God to be realized within a community of faith. It encourages God's people to come together for worship, pastoral teaching, and account-ability. (Hebrews 10:19-25)

| 10. "Broke bread in their homes" | The central nature of home and family to God's work on earth. |

Ministry Principle: A New Testament church believes and teaches that the home is the center of redemptive ministry. It holds to the conviction that home-based ministry is an order, and that loving family relationships are a cornerstone in God's plan. It encourages God's people to make their home a place of ministry and their family life an example of God's love through hospitality. (Joshua 24:15)

| 11. "Praising God" | The appropriate response of a human heart filled with God's Spirit. |

Ministry Principle: A New Testament church believes and teaches that the primary purpose of man is to worship God. It holds to the conviction that if mankind ever learns anything in life, he will learn to worship God out of his whole heart. It encourages God's people to see worship as a way of life as well as a corporate experience. (Psalms 34:1)

| 12. "Enjoying the favor of all the people" | The way outsiders felt about what is going on inside the hearts of "God's people." |

Ministry Principle: A New Testament church believes and teaches the importance of our behavior, never bringing reproach to the name of our God. It holds to serving God in the beauty of holiness. It encourages God's people to live out their faith in essentials with unity, and in nonessentials with charity. (Matthew 5:16)

I have been using the term "New Testament church" throughout this discussion of Acts 2:42-47. The use of this term is not to imply something exclusive or limited to a concept of the church that forsakes the foundations of the Old Covenant – quite the contrary. As was the actual Jewishness of the early church, we have no other place to begin our understanding of following Jesus together apart from the Old Testament record.

When the church was born in Jerusalem on that Pentecost feast day, God wasn't doing something different – He was doing something new!

TRANSITIONAL PARAGRAPHS

Some Bible scholars have identified a unique style of writing used by Luke as he organized his thoughts to give us the gospel of Luke and The Acts of the Apostles. The inspiration of the Holy Spirit gave him recall and accuracy, but also a very readable and well organized style.

The technique employed is called by some "transitional paragraphs." They are strategically placed throughout the two books. In fact, when all of them are identified and placed together in a contiguous listing, the experience of reading them is almost like reading a condensed version of the highlights of the life of Jesus Christ, the formation of the church in Israel, and the extension of the church through the missionary adventures of Paul.

For example, the section of Acts given to the formation of the church in Israel, primarily Jerusalem, is found in the first seven chapters of Acts. Identifying Luke's transitional paragraphs in that section of God's Word reads quickly and summarizes approximately seven or eight years of activity in the earliest days of the emergence of the church.

Let me give it to you, identifying each paragraph in the margin. This simplified and concise reading underscores what I consider to be some of the most important qualities of a New Testament church that desperately need to be put into practice in today's church.

Paragraph One: Acts 2:42-47

ACTS 2:42   They devoted themselves to the apostles' teaching, and to the fellowship, to the breaking of bread and to prayer.

ACTS 2:43   Everyone was filled with awe, and many wonders and miraculous signs were done by the apostles.

ACTS 2:44   All the believers were together and had everything in common.

ACTS 2:45   Selling their possessions and goods, they gave to anyone as he had need.

ACTS 2:46   Every day they continued to meet together with glad and sincere hearts,

ACTS 2:47   praising God and enjoying the favor of all the people. And the Lord added to their number daily those who were being saved.

Paragraph Two: Acts 4:32-35

ACTS 4:32   All the believers were one in heart and mind. Not one claimed that any of his possessions was his own, but they shared everything they had.

ACTS 4:33   With great power the apostles continued to testify to the resurrection of the Lord Jesus, and much grace was with them all.

ACTS 4:34   There were no needy persons among them. For from time to time those who owned lands or houses sold them, and brought the money from the sales

ACTS 4:35   and put it at the apostles' feet, and it was distributed to anyone as he had need.

Paragraph Three: Acts 5:12-16

ACTS 5:12   The apostles performed many miraculous signs and wonders among the people. And all the believers used to meet in Solomon's Colonnade.

ACTS 5:13   No one else dared join them, even though they were highly regarded by the people.

ACTS 5:14   Nevertheless, more and more men and women believed in the Lord and were added to their number.

ACTS 5:15   As a result people brought the sick into the streets and laid them on beds and mats so that at least Peter's shadow might fall on some of them as he passed by.

ACTS 5:16   Crowds gathered also from the towns around Jerusalem, bringing their sick and those tormented by evil spirits, and all of them were healed.

Paragraph Four: Acts 5:42

ACTS 5:42   Day after day in the temple courts and from house to house, they never stopped teaching and proclaiming the good news that Jesus is the Christ.

Paragraph Five: Acts 6:7-8

ACTS 6:7   So the word of God spread. The number of disciples in Jerusalem increased rapidly, and a large number of priests became obedient to the faith.

ACTS 6:8   Now Stephen, a man full of God's grace and power, did great wonders and miraculous signs among the people.

Paragraph Six: Acts 8:1-4

ACTS 8:1   And Saul was there giving approval to his death (Stephen). On that day a great persecution broke out against the church at Jerusalem, and all except the apostles were scattered throughout Judea and Samaria.

ACTS 8:2   Godly men buried Stephen and mourned deeply for him.

ACTS 8:3   But Saul began to destroy the church. Going from house to house, he dragged off men and women and put them in prison.

ACTS 8:4   Those who had been scattered preached the word wherever they went.

Well, you will have to agree with me, it makes for some very exciting reading. But let's take note of the characteristics of this Jerusalem church. Could it be that all we read here is to be expected in our churches today? Let's not be too quick to answer that question. I think as we go along together, we find some pretty convincing proof that the Lord has not changed His mind about what His church is supposed to be doing and being in each generation.

THE TRANSITIONAL PARAGRAPHS REVISITED

Let's see what they have to say to us about what a New Testament church looks like:

Paragraph	Characteristic
Acts 2:42-47	Unity and Devotion
Acts 4:32-35	Sharing and Compassionate Acts
Acts 5:12-16	Healings and Miracles
Acts 5:42	Teaching and Proclamation
Acts 6:7-8	Faithfulness and Reputation
Acts 8:1-4	Suffering and Persecution

Acts 2:42-47—Unity and Devotion

This paragraph has already been discussed earlier in the chapter, but the key here is the united and devoted nature of the early community of believers. They believed very much in what they were doing. There was no game playing here, and their relationship to the Body of Christ was a primary commitment.

Acts 4:32-35—Sharing and Compassion

This passage of Scripture has had a life-changing effect upon my family and me. It was here that we learned about people who cared so much about each other that they did what was necessary to help each other out. They prayed, and then it seems they started living the answers to those very same prayers.

Two statements are absolutely mind-boggling in this paragraph: *"All the believers were one in heart and mind,"* and *"There were no needy person among them"* (verse 32). The first speaks of a selflessness the Holy Spirit had worked in their hearts that we know little of today. Somehow they had come to a point in their understanding of God's grace, where they really believed and lived like they understood that everything they called their own was actually God's. As a result of that kind of commonality, they were utterly united – joined at the heart and in their understanding of their equality before God.

The second statement in verse 34 is not an exaggeration. Remember, this is God's inspired Word, not the product of an overly zealous evangelistic report. Think of it – *"no needy person among them."* This is a dream and goal of all ministering people, but somehow eludes us constantly. This is a key to New Testament church life: people involved in meeting the full range of one another's needs through constant and vigilant awareness of these needs by means of some kind of an accountability structure of communication. This scripture is a possibility today or it would not be in the Bible. However, the structure currently employed by most churches does not provide the relational avenues for such ministry to take place.

Acts 5:12-16—Healings and Miracles

Are we open to this today, or have we lamely opted for the "cop-out" that this "signs and wonders" business is a thing of the past? We need to decide whether we want to dedicate our lives to developing a "rationale for impotence" or are we going to "contend for the authentic" manifestation of the power of God in His church today.

If you want to contend, then understand that it is not as "tidy" as it might sound. When a church contends for healings and miracles, then sick folks and tormented people have a habit of showing up. Do you want that? We all have our preconceived idea of the kind of congregation we would like to lead or the type of church we would like to attend. It doesn't usually include lots of people with major physical, mental, or emotional problems.

A New Testament church that has made up its mind that it is contending for the supernatural power of God to be at work in people's lives and bodies must also be ready to contend for a New Testament order and discipline. "Signs and wonders" must not be connected with disorderliness or emotionalism. I personally resent the implication that in order to believe that God could or would heal and deliver people today would require one to "hang their brains on a hook."

Acts 5:42—Teaching and Proclamation

It is important to note here that there were two dynamics of assembly in this early church: temple and house. Both were important. Both were consistent. Both were the scene of the teaching and proclaiming of the Word of God. In this day and age of a mindset where there is a clear line of demarcation of church and state, we have done the same to our houses – separation of church and home – one set of rules and dynamics for the church building, and another set of expectations for our places of residence. This attitude is severely limiting the potential of the church today and will be thoroughly discussed in another chapter of this book.

There is definitely a place and a role for both dynamics, but it must not be one or the other; nor should the home life suffer in order for the "temple" program to be served.

Acts 6:7-8—Fruitfulness and Reputation

It is important to see that the harmony and blessing described in this paragraph only came after a very difficult time in the church. Chapter 5 and the earlier part of chapter 6 share with us a serious crisis in this baby church. However, it is not left to fester – it was confronted. It was not treated lightly, but the Lord was consulted in prayer, difficult decisions were made, and a corrective procedure and plan was initiated. It was in the wake of that kind of sensitive and decisive leadership that verse 7 is possible. We would all like to see this verse happening:

1. The Word of God spreading.
2. Number of disciples increasing.
3. Large number of "outsiders" were believing.

Victory never comes without some kind of a struggle. The progress described here was possible because sin had been dealt with properly, authority had been upheld, and unity was allowed to once again dominate everyone's heart. The atmosphere in which the Holy Spirit moves with power is an atmosphere of love and unity. This is the ultimate "glory" or manifested presence of God. The growing reputation of the Jerusalem church was the actual living of Jesus' commandment to *"love one another,"* and the fulfillments of His promise that *"all men will know that you are my disciples if you love one another"* (John 13:35).

Acts 8:1-4—Suffering and Persecution

We probably do not like to hear it, but suffering and persecution are a consequence of living like the New Testament. The church that refuses to be pinned down to a cultural or traditional model of how it will operate will be maligned and misunderstood, particularly by other believers. The church that refuses to be pinned down to a cultural or traditional definition will make such outstanding inroads into the kingdom of darkness that it will experience some degree of opposition that will, at times, bring with it pain and suffering. The enemy of men's and women's souls does not want the church "alive and well." This is the cost of what we are talking about in this book. One must count the cost before doing anything with this challenge. All I can say at this point is, "Hear the word of the Lord."

> *"But thanks be to God! He gives us the victory through our Lord Jesus Christ. Therefore, my dear brothers, stand firm. Let nothing move you. Always give yourself fully to the work of the Lord because you know that your labor in the Lord is not in vain."*
> —1 Corinthians 15:57-58

CHAPTER 2

. . . .

WHAT DOES YOUR CHURCH LOOK LIKE?

AS A YOUNGSTER growing up in Oakland, California, most of my playmates were Roman Catholic. The kids I played with were a part of "Our Lady of Lourdes" parish and attended the parochial school there. Being the only Protestant on the block, I was often perplexed with their talk about their religion.

In fact, I was very frightened of the Catholic faith and the "Our Lady of Lourdes" church. You see, to my young mind the rituals and the liturgy, so meaningful and so beautiful to my Catholic playmates, were a deep, dark mystery. "Strange things go on in a Catholic church," I often thought. Sometimes, I would walk by the always open door of the foreboding and steepled building, so unlike the simpler evangelical edifice we attended, straining to catch a glimpse of the candlelight or a priest or nun moving about doing their mysterious duties.

Sometimes, I pondered what seemed to be the complicated customs of the Mass and knew that I never could go in there. I would not know what to do or when to do it, and of course everyone would know that I was not a Catholic. Probably, with every eye critically focused upon me, I imagined, they would throw me out of the place.

I suppose my Catholic neighbors felt pretty much the same way about the place our family worshipped, but that didn't occur to me at the time. I did notice that my many invitations to attend Sunday school were always turned down.

Lots of misunderstandings and misconceptions about church exist both then and now. We continue to miss the point. The church is not a place. The church is people – people who have been washed in the blood of Jesus.

As long as we continue to allow church to be defined by real estate and architecture, and the liturgies, ordinances, and traditions that take place inside, we will continue to tragically limit the possibilities Jesus had in mind when He "invented" the church.

FIELD OR FORCE

A church that is tightly wrapped in a restricting institutional definition tends to become maintenance-oriented and defensively postured. The church Jesus spoke of in Matthew 16 (when He commended Peter's faith and prophesied of a people who would make a similar confession) was dynamic in nature. It was never content to languish in sedimentary defensiveness, but was aggressive; reaching out in Jesus' name to those who, like the little boy in Oakland, California, peered through doors and windows of religious monuments wondering, "What's going on in there?"

My friend and colleague Jerry Cook here in the Seattle, Washington, area was one of the first to introduce a concept of church that forever shattered for me the mold of defensive posturing. This concept is best described as our mind-set regarding the church compared metaphorically to a "field" or a "force."

THE CHURCH AS A FIELD

Those who see the church as a place have the concept that church is a piece of real estate where people "come." When the church is perceived as a place, then an inordinate amount of time, energy, and money is directed at the care of that edifice and its environs. Usually, more members are involved in ministries that take place "at the church" than those involved in ministry beyond the four walls of the building. There is a tendency to conceptualize the mission of the church as being defined by a time-space definition of church:

Time: "We have church at such-and-such a time on such-and-such a day."

Space: "Our church is located on such-and-such a street."

The "field" is a place to get people to come at a certain time in order to "have church." Commonly held expressions that represent this concept of church, and by their very articulation limit the church's effectiveness, are:

"Lets go to church!"

"When is the church going to do something about that?"

"When is church over?"

"We have to get more people to come to church."

These expressions are typical of the "church-as-a-field" way of thinking. Constantly grasping for bigger, better, more fascinating ways of getting people packed into rows in a building, and then complaining when overcrowding becomes an inconvenience to our worship experience. Because there is a serious dichotomy in this thinking, people begin to develop two realities: 1) a church reality with a certain set of protocols and regulations; and 2) another set of rules and rituals for the rest of life lived outside the church building. This kind of dualism creates double standards, confusion, and even hypocrisies when left unabated.

THE CHURCH AS A FORCE

We need to see the church as people. The best definition I have ever heard for the church is: "Anyone who has been washed in the blood of Jesus." Pure and simple, the force mentality sees the church everywhere at once and not confined to a street corner, or a particular service schedule. No longer can a power failure, a snowstorm, or the chicken pox stop this kind of church – people working, people playing, children studying, and men and women going about their everyday lives having church.

That's right, having church! Worshipping, sharing, praying, and growing wherever they are – this is the church without walls. Yes, we gather often for corporate meetings. Yes, we have a place to meet and come in out of the rain. But church is never over. Evangelism is more than a special evangelistic "service." Ministry far exceeds something that can only take place on a platform or in a classroom. The church becomes a force moving out into the community with God's grace and love rather than begging people to come in.

BE JESUS TO PEOPLE

As a small boy, that neighborhood Catholic church symbolized something cold, unfriendly, and rigid. It dared me to qualify for admittance. The gospel demands that the people of God must not hide behind our buildings, liturgies, and doctrines. We must go! The Body of Christ does not look like places or things. The Body of Christ is a living organism made up of common and ordinary people like you and me. Together we represent our Lord Jesus. He looks like us, not the things we build or the way we dress on Sunday. I began to challenge our congregation as we learned these things to "be Jesus to people." Almost every benediction included this admonition. We began to understand that the church is people, and the only Jesus anyone in our town was going to see that week (unless the Lord chose to return) was going to be the Jesus they saw in each one of us.

WHAT DOES THE CHURCH LOOK LIKE?

After considering the implications of those New Testament passages of scripture that present the church as being like a human body – more specifically being the visible and current representation of the Lord Jesus on this planet – we must ask ourselves the question: "What does our church look like?" We are not talking about architecture or order of services. Believing that the "force" model we discussed earlier is a more accurate summation of the Lord's teaching on the church than a "field" model, we must answer the question in light of the value and effect of the individual and collective human lives of the redeemed. In other words, what is really happening through the lives of the congregation's members? Does our church look like the church we read about in the book of Acts or does it resemble something more stylized to fit our time or our culture? The early church was a force if there ever was one. It was a "church on the loose!" We will do well to follow its dynamic example.

THE EARLY CHURCH AS A FORCE...
THE CHURCH ON THE LOOSE!

The first eight chapters of the book of Acts give us a compressed look at what many Bible scholars believe was

THE CHURCH HAS LEFT THE BUILDING

a period of approximately eight years. Over those years, we see a church emerging out of Pentecost that becomes very viable in its influence and impact upon Jerusalem, Judea, and Samaria. Viability is a factor that every local church should have as a goal:

VIABILITY: "The ability to stay alive."

When this term is used relative to human life, it simply means that the individual is capable of maintaining life outside of the womb. As I use the term in this chapter, my definition is: "When the corporate dynamics of a body of believers have grown to such a point that the quality of their spirituality and their fellowship has a living effect upon the community that surrounds their meeting place." No longer is their church simply occupying a prominent corner on a city map. No longer do the majority of people within the community walk or drive by wondering what that place is about. No longer does the community continue on with its date with eternal destiny unaware of what the people in the church building on the corner are like or what they believe.

We prayed that the Lord of the church would send us people from all walks of life. The Danville church represented an interesting cross-section of the kinds of people that comprised our community. We learned that as we began to pray for a specific aspect of the community, He would send people from that aspect of the community to come into the fellowship. For example, when we began to seriously intercede for the educational system and encouraged the parents of children enrolled in public schools to get actively involved in their children's school, we began to see a growing number of school teachers, staff members, and administrators coming to the Lord and becoming a part of the church.

This is not magic of some kind. We learned that specific prayer resulted in specific answers. I remember the same thing happening when we would target specific neighborhoods or districts in prayer. The best way I know to get your church viably involved in community issues and politics is through prayer, followed by key members getting involved. For us, this resulted in evangelistic and friendship contacts that brought our church right into the mainstream of these forces and interest groups within the community.

The sidelines are no place to sit in days like today. While I do not for a moment believe that a great church is built on singling out issues and championing them, it is vitally important for individual members of a congregation to get involved in every segment of the community. A healthy church reaches every part of the socio-economic ladder of the community in which it serves, and encourages its people to actively engage themselves in those things that affect the way the community evolves as a part of our society.

This can be exemplified by church members like Sally, who volunteers to work a few mornings a week at her daughter's elementary school; Tom, who leaves his business early fall afternoons to help coach a high school football team; Agnes, whose senior years are partially fulfilled by her volunteer work at the local hospital. (How many lives have been comforted and spiritually focused because she came by distributing newspapers and magazines?)

I think of Mary and her conviction to see Christians registered to vote and Frank, whose responsibilities as a busy executive did not prohibit him from working actively with the crisis pregnancy outreach our church helped get started. I recall Betty, who became a key leader in the Chamber of Commerce, and a number of others who spent a night or two a month at local jails ministering to inmates. The list goes on, and I think you get the idea.

Local church leadership that seeks viability releases the manpower of a congregation into the community, rather than attempting to harness and control it for "in-house" purposes. The release of God's people into community involvement is a more accurate interpretation of the Great Commission of Jesus Christ than simply trying everything possible to get people clustered around pulpits to hear great sermons. In my opinion, if fifty percent of a congregation is involved in the maintenance of a church program, then at least as many should be channeled into more outreach-oriented ministries.

The "viability factor," in effect, means that a local church is affecting the way a community behaves itself. The invitation of the Lord of the church for His people to be "salt" and "light" has been accepted. Schools are affected through believers' conscientious involvement in the classrooms, offices, and playgrounds. Business is affected as Christian merchants, employers, and employees see their jobs and work places as opportunities to worship the Lord through honest practices and godly attitudes. Neighborhoods are affected as believers' residences become "house churches" and church members put a policy of hospitality and neighborliness into practice.

D. Richard Halverson, former chaplain of the United States Senate and former pastor of Fourth Presbyterian Church of Bethesda, Maryland, was once casually asked where his church was. His enlightened response to the question perfectly illustrates my point. "Where is Fourth Presbyterian?" he responded. "Why, it's delivering milk, teaching school, practicing law, and going to the grocery store. Our church is all over town right now." I think the questioner was expecting an address, but, in fact, received a more purely correct answer to his query. This pastor understood what the church really looks like – it looks like people. Where the church really is, is wherever those people are. He understood that the church is a "force" and not a "field."

When "viability" is attained, a community experiences the redemptive power of Jesus Christ as His church moves out into everyday life, understanding that all they are and do is an act of worship. They're "having church!"

The "frontlines" of community viability and impact are found at our places of residence. If we are going to "have church" any place at all, we must be sure to "have it" at home! Let me tell you an amusing story about how we got started having home meetings.

CHAPTER 3

BRINGING IT ALL HOME

I T WAS WEDNESDAY. The previous Sunday, our first in
Danville, we had invited those present to our home that
evening for our very first home meeting. We were excited,
wondering who would come and what God would do, but
we were also perplexed. How do you have a "church" at
home? You see, our twelve years of experience in full-time
ministry had, up until that point, never included a religious
service in any kind of private residence. We simply had
nothing to go on. We knew that it was time to put our Acts
2:42-47 model to work, and "house-to-house" was on the
agenda. Unfortunately, the Scriptures were mute (or a least
we thought so at the time) on how to conduct a "church"
at home.

After talking about it for a while, we simply did what
we knew. Couch, chair, and coffee table were removed and
replaced by rows of folding chairs produced from our garage.
Where previously a table lamp had perched, now, in all of
its glory, was our newly purchased overhead projector. Of
course in order to project images of songs and choruses it

was necessary to remove one of our paintings from the wall. Finishing touches included an offering basket nestled in a corner, printed materials lying on every other chair, and of course my lectern. Well, you can see the Hayfords were ready to HAVE church – church in their home, that is.

I don't know what the twenty or so people thought about the arrangement they found inside our house, for they were always gracious, and most of them were doing this for the first time too. But as we look back through the years at our first few home meetings, we laugh at ourselves. Our concept of church was so predictable, so incredibly limited. It had taken enormous courage to open our home for people to come and do "church things." Faced with providing them an environment for worship, fellowship, and spiritual instruction forced us to think that duplicating the facilities we frequented on Sundays (we call them churches) would be the appropriate thing to do, so we did.

It was awkward – chairs scratching our hardwood floors not made for this kind of traffic, heads and necks at unusual angles, trying to see around lamp shades and plants to obediently read the overhead images prescribing their singing. I felt silly behind a lectern in my own living room, and something about the whole "service" did not ring true to us, as my wife and I would review the gathering each week after our guests had left for home.

"Let's stop having church in here and just have people over to our house," we decided. "We can still do 'church things,' but do it in a 'home way.'" We concluded that we would throw away the institutional mold when it came to meetings in our home. We set out from that day to stop entertaining people in our house and start showing hospitality.

The following Wednesday when our fledging congregation arrived, they found our living room looking like a normal one. I have often wondered if some thought that we lived in a house that remained in the ecclesiastical configuration day in and day out – the way they found it on Wednesday nights. That to me was a funny thought, and I had to chuckle inside thinking about someone's relief when they walked into their new pastor's house and saw that he and his family lived much the way they did.

Now they could relax in our home. This is what we had wanted all along – lamps in their places, things back on the wall where they belonged. ("Oh, they do have some normal tastes in home decorating!") A few must have breathed with relief. Overhead projector, offering basket, and all the other accoutrements of "church" were nowhere to be seen. "Welcome to our home," I began that night. We were smiling at each other, my wife and I, from across the room. This was right. This was real. No longer would we have to make our house like "God's house." We finally realized that it was His all along, and now we were going to share it with our friends – as is.

And you know something? As I recall, that night we "had church." I mean, everything we could have ever hoped for in terms of the people's response to the Word of God, the power of the praise, the quality of the ministry to one another, was so satisfying, so complete. We had finally "come home."

HOME MINISTRIES

From this first group that met in our home, we learned much about how the church could gather "from house to house, breaking bread with gladness and singleness of hearts." It is important to note that the primary leader's family was willing to be the "guinea pig." Our home was the "test tube." We learned lessons about biblical hospitality first hand so that we were able to teach and reproduce those lessons in the lives and homes of the people we led and served. We found that it is one thing to request people to open their homes to the people of God and their neighbors, but it is entirely another thing to train the people in the most effective use of their residence in ministry. This requires more than theory – it requires experience.

Some of the important guidelines we gleaned from the first few years of welcoming people into our home on a weekly basis are as follows:

1. Leadership is the key to effective home meetings.
2. Family members must not feel "displaced."
3. Hospitality should be shared by the group.
4. Household rules become the group's rules as well.
5. The entire group should share a "good neighbor" policy.
6. Never "play church" at a home meeting; it could be a fatal mistake.

Let's discuss each of these guidelines in more detail, so you and your group need not make some of the mistakes we did.

LEADERSHIP IS THE KEY

Leadership is, of course, the key in virtually every aspect of ministry. I have heard of many churches that started home ministries as a program of their church, giving little attention to the training of the men and women who would be leading the groups. In many cases, trouble erupted within the church because of divisive attitudes and personality, and doctrinal problems that were born and bred within the small groups. I can understand why, after these kinds of difficulties, more than one pastor has vowed to "never have a home group in this church again!" The release of ministry from underneath the immediate purvey of a pastor's personal involvement will always include a certain degree of risk. But that risk need not be as volatile as some would believe if proper development of leadership is the first priority in implementing a small group or home group strategy of ministry.

Our aim in developing home meetings is to allow people's homes to serve as regular places of assembly for the church family and for those from the community that they invite. It greatly multiplies the church's effectiveness in pastoral care, as well as evangelistic outreach. Many who will come to these smaller, less threatening gatherings in homes would never "darken the door" of our sanctuaries and auditoriums.

This aim cannot be realized without qualified and reliable leadership. Second Timothy 2:2 states: *"And the things you have heard me say in the presence of many witnesses entrust to reliable men who will also be qualified to teach others."* This concise definition of discipleship became my basis for preparing others to lead home meetings.

The two words that are particularly important with regards to leadership development in this text are "reliable" and "qualified." The first word implies relational account-ability – a character trait. The second word speaks of the individual's ability, both spiritually and intellectually. Training home group leaders is a process of delegation. In delegating, three qualities are being entrusted to the disciple or "apprentice": **responsibility**, **authority**, and **accountability**. It is in the proper understanding of these qualities and the careful handling of them that leadership is properly transferred and God's people are faithfully served. When the one with delegating privilege overlooks any one of these qualities, there will be problems. (See Appendix II and V)

As time went by and the church grew, the number of small groups multiplied. Our first group soon became four. Two years later there were ten. And as the years progressed, the number of groups grew proportionately to the total congregation's growth. In order to apply these principles of leadership discipleship, all leaders were required to meet with me every Friday morning at 6:00 A.M. to study the Scriptures, bear each other's burdens, and be accountable to one another. Never let the size, geography, or any other complexity allow the relationship between leaders to suffer from neglect. It must remain the highest priority.

RESPONSIBILITY

In the case at hand the responsibility is great. The pastoral care of God's people is at stake. In asking an individual to serve as a leader of a group of people within the church, and those they touch in their neighborhood, we are asking a lot of a person.

This person is probably already very busy with family, job, and church. Be sure they are not over committed. Help them to evaluate their priorities, making certain that this new responsibility can be accepted without doing serious damage to other, more important, responsibilities already stretched to the breaking point.

If one accepts responsibility for a home group, be sure they fully understand the importance of what they are taking on, and clearly understand the "job description" before saying "yes." It is important, if the individual is married, that their spouse and children understand what their family member is "getting into" so they can enthusiastically support them. Make the potential leader's family a part of the decision, for more than likely they are the ones who will sacrifice the most. In preparing a potential home leader for this responsibility, I have stressed to them that their assignment carries with it five elements:

1. **FRIENDSHIP:** Small groups should provide opportunity for people to be able to casually and meaningfully acknowledge one another's presence. Building rapport and intimacy within the group is one of the leader's responsibilities.
2. **WORSHIP:** Small groups should provide opportunity for people to acknowledge God's presence, power, and potential in their gathering. Leading people in praise provides an atmosphere that facilitates the moving of God's Spirit. A group leader should find someone to provide this kind of leadership if they are unable to do so themselves.
3. **FELLOWSHIP:** Small groups should provide opportunity for people to acknowledge one another's needs so they can be met by the grace of God. Fellowship implies commonality. In a small group, leadership develops an attitude of "all things common" – common needs through open and honest sharing; common resources through open and honest prayers; and common ministry through allowing the gifts of the Holy Spirit to be shared in the group.
4. **DISCIPLESHIP:** Small groups should provide opportunity for people to be taught from God's Word by the one appointed to do so at that meeting. Leadership comes prepared to feed God's people a well-organized, well-prepared study of God's Word in keeping with the text prescribed by pastoral leadership.

5. **WORKMANSHIP:** Small groups should provide opportunity for God's people to respond to what the Lord is saying throughout the meeting. A leader must learn to provide opportunity for responses of repentance and commitment through personal ministry.

Responsibilities of leadership vary from church to church and group to group. The above responsibilities seem to me to be the highest priority in a group whose assignment is pastoral in nature. Other more specific responsibilities must be defined, modeled, and taught.

For example, home group leadership for us included instruction in: "How to Serve Holy Communion," "How to Deal with People Who Dominate a Meeting," "How to Start a Discussion," "How to Lead Worship," and others from time to time as questions arose.

Leadership was nurtured in the following ways:

1. First, all group leaders were to have a relationship with the pastor and be members of the church.
2. All group leaders attended a six-week training session.
3. All group leaders were committed to our "Standard for Leaders." (See Appendix II)
4. All group leaders spent at least one year attending a home group before leading one.
5. All group leaders were discipled or sponsored by another group leader who recommended them.
6. All group leaders met with the pastor weekly for teaching and prayer as a group. This was mandatory.

7. All group leaders were committed to dealing with the same text as the other groups on a given week for continuity within the entire church.
8. All group leaders were willing to reproduce themselves by discipling future leaders for other groups to come or as their replacement.

AUTHORITY

All of us know the frustration of being asked to perform a task but to not be given sufficient authority to properly fulfill the assignment. Empowerment is of great importance to all who desire to really get the job done. However, power and authority are dangerous when placed in the wrong hands. Sufficient time must be taken in the discipling process to determine how an individual will handle authority – both under it and how it is used in others' lives. It is the true heart of a servant that Jesus seeks in spiritual leadership.

My mentor, Dr. Don McGregor, (a servant-leader if ever I have known one) has taught me much about serving God's people. Here is a list of "Ten Basic Qualities Essential for Home Group Leaders" that he prepared and that I include here with his permission:

Home Group Leaders Should:
1. Have a vital commitment to the local church body walking in submission "one to another."
2. Be a willing student of the Word and disciplined in prayer.
3. Demonstrate and confess spiritual growth and life in the Spirit.
4. Be building strong, loving relationships within one's family and with others beyond the immediate family circle.

5. Have his/her home life in order – whether married or single.
6. Willingly practice hospitality.
7. Evidence ability to lead a small group around a common meal, discussion of spiritual matters, or lead a prayer time.
8. Be willing and ready to invest the necessary time for home group meetings, group prayer, fellowship, and training sessions.
9. Be willing to care for and bear the burden of ten to twenty other people.
10. Have a functional understanding and appreciation of spiritual gifts and ministry.

Authority is expressed safely when the one having that power understands the ultimate authority of Jesus Christ and the biblical, ordered, and accepted chain of command within the church. Ultimately, the only authority an individual has is that given to them, and that which is lived out within the confines of their own marriage and family.

ACCOUNTABILITY

People are busy. Sometimes communication with one another is far briefer than we wish. In our day and age, relationships need management – there is little time for them to just "happen." The following material is designed to facilitate accountable relationships between leaders and those they lead. This model is not meant to enforce a relationship that is legalistic and ultimately destructive. It is meant only to enable busy people to stay within a framework of relationship that provides time for communication, support, and accountability.

GUIDELINES FOR SMALL GROUPS

Small groups must have a focus. Some are prayer groups, some are discussion or support groups. In fact, there are any number of reasons small groups could be meeting. Small groups must have consistent intervals. How often will the groups meet? Are they primary to the ministry of the church or are they treated as expendable afterthoughts?

OUR PHILOSOPHY FOR SMALL GROUPS IS "PASTORAL CARE"

A. **WORSHIP:** Psalms 100:2-4 indicates an attitude of appreciation and an attitude of adoration that are important qualities in coming into the Lord's presence in company. We know, beyond any shadow of a doubt, that the moving of the Holy Spirit in a meeting is facilitated with praise. Praise unites, praise edifies, and praise exalts Jesus Christ. (John 12:32; James 4:8; Psalm 22:3)

1. Corporate praise requires direction.
2. Corporate praise requires an objective.
3. Corporate praise is to be creative.
4. Teach worship, exhort worship, practice worship.

B. **FELLOWSHIP:** Philippians 2:3-4 indicates an attitude of genuine concern and compassion that is common-place in a truly Spirit-filled community of believers. Adequate opportunity needs to be given so people can minister to one another's needs. It is this kind of body life that will make it possible for a church's needs to be met. (Acts 2:44; 4:34; Galatians 6:2)

1. Body life requires teaching.
2. Body life requires suggestions.
3. Body life requires time.
4. Teach body life, exhort body life, and practice body life.

C. **INTERCESSION:** First Timothy 2:1 indicates an attitude of absolute dependence upon God for His intervention in the affairs of man; realizing, however, that God has given man dominion on this earth, and our petitions release the Lord to work on our behalf and on behalf of others. (Psalm 122:6; Luke 11:1; 1 Timothy 2:8)

1. Intercession requires conviction.
2. Intercession requires coordination.
3. Intercession requires consistency.
4. Teach intercession, exhort intercession, practice intercession.

D. **COMMUNION:** Acts 2:46 indicates to us that the Lord's Table was a very important part of the gatherings of the early church. Remembering the Lord's death through the elements of bread and wine constantly bring the focus of our fellowship upon its most important elements. It centers on Jesus Christ – dead, buried, risen, and reigning from the right hand of the Father. (1 Corinthians 11:23-30)

1. Communion requires creativity.
2. Communion requires self-evaluation.
3. Communion requires unit.
4. Teach communion, exhort communion, practice communion.

E. **TEACHING:** Second Timothy 2:2 gives us the New Testament pattern for discipleship. You, as a leader, will be called upon to break the Word of God to the hungry people assembled. The Word will find a lodging place in the heart of each one who has been led through the other components of a New Testament gathering as listed above. (2 Timothy 2:15; 2 Timothy 3:16)

1. Teaching requires preparation.
2. Teaching requires learning.
3. Teaching requires listening.
4. Teaching requires repetition.
5. Disciple teachers, exhort teachers, practice teaching.

A FACILITATING STRUCTURE FOR SMALL GROUPS

It seems to me that authentic ministry must be measurable and accountable. As a congregation grows, the need for intimacy among the members grows. People do not want to get "lost in the crowd." As pastors, we should be doing everything we can to eliminate a "crowd mentality" in our churches and encourage a "community mentality" instead. Community implies familiarity, mutual responsibility, and awareness of one another's needs.

I am convinced that this is not possible in a typical church model that "has services" rather than putting people in touch with each other.

Small groups make New Testament ministry possible in such a way that people actually feel a part of the ministry rather than a spectator of it. The small group provides an opportunity within the main structure of the church for the following dynamics to take place:

1. **DISCIPLE LEADERSHIP:** A network of smaller groups makes it necessary for leadership of these groups to be shared by a number of the members. This releases a multiplication of involvement that spreads the burden and increases the vision. When leadership is released, it broadens the base on which the Lord will build His church.

    NOTE: It is necessary for the primary leader/teacher to develop a meaningful relationship with these people and to adequately train them before releasing them into leadership. Discipleship delegates responsibility, authority, and accountability.

2. **DEVELOP RELATIONSHIPS:** Allowing people to join small groups will result in the development of personal relationships – the primary ingredient in a strong body of believers. The primary need of most church members is the love and acceptance that comes to them through meaningful relationships.

    NOTE: We are looking for people who can make a real commitment to their church family. This comes through important relationships, not just key doctrines or interesting programs. We must give people "up close" opportunities to commit themselves to each other.

3. **EXPOSE NEEDS:** The striking example of the Jerusalem church is that they were a group where

"no one had a need" is challenging to say the least. Just think of it, a church where everyone's needs were met or in the process of being met. Small groups are a safe place for people to be really honest with each other about their needs.

NOTE: It seems to me that we cannot begin to be a need-meeting community unless a constant and accepting forum is provided where people can talk "out loud" about where they hurt and what they lack. We must provide this opportunity for our people. In doing this, we release the gifts and resources of the Body of Christ like a great wave of love and compassion as people respond to one another.

4. **STIR UP SPIRITUAL GIFTS:** In the process of meeting each other's needs and "bearing one another's burdens," the grace of God is shared through the gifts of the Holy Spirit.

    NOTE: The gifts of the Holy Spirit should be encouraged to be in operation in small groups. Ordered and disciplined by well-trained leaders, these gifts should flow beautifully in the smaller setting where accountability and follow up are possible.

5. **FACILITATES GROWTH AND EXPANSION:** Small groups that are geographically spread throughout the region of influence of a local church encourage involvement of those who live some distance from the primary meeting place. They also become starting points for church-planting efforts.

NOTE: Leaders should carefully plan where small groups should meet so as to provide accessibility for members throughout their "sphere of influence." Encourage involvement at the closest location, but never insist on it.

The potential of releasing a congregation into being a church without walls does not only involve home meetings throughout a city, such as I have described in this chapter. It involves families learning how to use their residences and their relationships redemptively. The following chapter will help you understand why the home and family are the primary building blocks God uses to build His church in any city or town.

CHAPTER 4

THE FAMILY, GOD'S PRIMARY BUILDING BLOCK

"Day after day, in the temple courts and from house to house they never stopped teaching and proclaiming the good news that Jesus is the Christ."

—Acts 5:42

"When she [Lydia] and the members of her household were baptized, she invited us to her home. 'If you consider me a believer in the Lord,' she said, 'come and stay at my house.' And she persuaded us."

—Acts 16:15

"Greet Priscilla and Aquilla...Greet also the church that meets at their house."

—Romans 16:3, 5

GOD HAD A BETTER IDEA

WHEN GOD DETERMINED that there would be mankind, He decided in His infinite wisdom the way in which man would live and perpetuate himself. Marriage, family –these were God's ideas. After all, He could have created us with entirely different instincts, capabilities, and desires. Our biology is the product of His heart, not the sum of our parts.

The Bible itself, for the most part, is a book about families. Story after story is about how people did or didn't get along with each other within the confines of family relationships, and how that affected the lives and history of many others. The New Testament Scriptures are "familial." The Gospels carefully disclose to us the family relationships of Jesus and the intimate nature of His relationship with His disciples. The lessons and sermons of our Savior invariably find their way back to an application that needs to be made "at home."

One of the clearest metaphors Jesus gave His disciples of what His church and His kingdom should resemble was the family. (Matthew 7:24, 12:25)

As the church unfolds before us in the Acts of the Apostles, we see a "family of faith" sharing together in a commonality rarely seen outside of the privacy and the intimacy of a natural family.

Colossians 3:12-21 (Please read before continuing.)

Traditionally, this passage of Scripture is read and taught as an epitome of church life and relationships in the institutional sense. In other words, this is the way people ought to treat each other "at church." However, there is much more intended here. While most English versions divide the section between verses 17 and 18 with notes suggesting a change in context from "church" to "home," I maintain that the entire passage belongs together as one. The familial exhortations of verses 18-21 clearly show us that the writer's intention is toward home life. This division of this text is only one example of our consistent error and persistent attitude that seeks to define the church as an entity separate from daily life, most of which is lived out in our homes.

GOD'S PURPOSE FOR HOME AND FAMILY

Of course, a book on this subject alone would not be enough, but allow me a few comments. It seems to me that if we can recover the purpose of home and family in our life and times, we will be well on our way to recovering the purpose of the church. The "household" is the major and fundamental "currency" in God's "economy." Home and family are close to God's heart, and anything He has created (including the church) must never violate it.

Among many things that could be said, I believe that two of the principle reasons or purposes God instituted family life are:

1. To visibly demonstrate and model His very nature.
2. To redeem mankind by raising up a "godly offspring."

THE HOME WHERE GOD IS ON DISPLAY

God has always used those things closest to us – those things we best understand – as "visual aids" to teach us about Him. Perhaps the most difficult lesson in life for all of us to know and understand is God Himself. The home and family were "invented" by God to help us learn of His very nature. What a different world this would be if we all would have learned about our Lord and Savior in the sanctity of our own homes!

The Godhead, its mysterious unity and obvious diversity of roles and responsibilities, is modeled in a home as oneness defined in roles and lived in intimacy. It is lived out by a husband and a wife in the presence of children. We learn of God's love and how to receive and express that while living together at home – at least that's the way it's supposed to be. Other important characteristics and attributes of God are best learned if experienced first within the family.

We cannot separate home and church. The early church did not. The church that is being restored today back to its basic and beginning values by the power of the Holy Spirit must understand that. The church looks like people living and loving each other twenty-four hours a day!

RAISING A GODLY OFFSPRING

Malachi 2:15 explains the heart of God with regard to Israel's role in redemptive history. We come to the end of the Old Testament, and tragically Israel has miserably failed in her commission to be the source of blessing to the entire world. Here in the final pages of the prophets we are made to understand the "why" of God's blessings and dealings with His people: *"because he was seeking godly offspring."* The final words of Malachi, the final words of the Old Testament falling off into the void between the Testaments – with the Messiah just "around the corner" – continue to promise that God's "idea," the family, was still the link that God would use to accomplish His plan of redemption. *"He will turn the hearts of the fathers to their children, and the hearts of the children to their fathers"* (Malachi 4:6).

There is, more than ever, a crying need for homes where mother and father see themselves as responsible for the spiritual life and growth of their children. The time has come for parents to take back their previously abdicated role as models of redeeming love. The home and family, as God ordained it, is to become the center of redemption – first to our own flesh and blood and then to those who live around us.

A DIFFERENT WAY OF THINKING

Christians today need to adjust their thinking about their home and family. Our culture has taught us to believe that we can shift our attention away from home and everything in the society would remain intact. In fact, everything is coming "unglued," and the catalyst that is missing is the home.

Today, indifferent attitudes towards marriage, disregard for authority, loss of moral absolutes, and the endless search of mankind for sensual fulfillment are the direct result of the disappearance of home life. Home life centers on God's Word and is committed to biblical values. The church today has "volunteered" to take over the biblical training of its children, mistakenly believing that the institutional church could do a better job. Parents have complied with the invitation by dropping their children off at preschools, Christian schools, Sunday schools, and kid's clubs, while they went off to work or to do other "more important" things that they needed to do with their time. As helpful and as well intentioned as these institutional solutions are, they are not the answer. The solution lies back at the hearth of home and family.

The institutional church is not to do for a family what God has ordained in His Word that a family is to do for themselves.

But this concept of home and family is so foreign to our way of defining church these days that it will never come without a change of thinking, especially on the part of fathers.

THREE THOUGHTS FOR HEADS OF HOUSES

If Satan had his way, we would all be living in pigpens, our children would be drug-dependent, and our marriages would be blown apart. The enemy of our souls is hitting God at His most critical point – the family. In order for this to change, heads of houses (men or women) need to start thinking in terms of their homes being more important in God's plan than they previously thought.

Instead of only "going to church" and dragging their children behind them, parents need to "be the church" at home with their children around them. This is not a call for the "evacuation" of institutional church – of course not. Parents wanting to live like the church of the book of Acts and see their church-life defining their culture rather than see their culture defining their church-life, should consider shifting their focus ever so slightly back towards home. Again, it will require a different way of thinking.

Conviction One: That home and family become the central focus of our lives.

Conviction Two: That home and family become the primary conservatory of biblical values.

Conviction Three: That home and family become the principle conveyor of salvation.

These three convictions deal with the average Christian family's response to the Great Commission of Jesus Christ found in Matthew 28:19-20.

We are dealing with the issues of spirituality, discipleship, and God's plan of redemption. A home-based response to this mandate would be different for most of us. It would require considerable change in the way we run our homes, and also great change in the way we organize our churches.

Institutional church dynamics and realities must become the same as what we do at home and vice-versa. Any other approach is a kind of hypocrisy that unbelievers and especially our children see in our lives. One set of rules and regulations for home and another set for church flies in the face of our Lord's mandate. Liturgies, politesse, programs, and creeds are important and have their place. But we must be asking ourselves the question: "Will it work at home?"

THE GREAT COMMISSION AND THE FAMILY

"Therefore go and make disciples of all nations, baptizing them in the name of the Father and of the Son and of the Holy Spirit, and teaching them to obey everything I have commanded you. And surely I will be with you always, to the very end of the age."
—Matthew 28:19-20

We obey the Great Commission (or disobey) every time we walk out the door of our home. We have lulled ourselves into a kind of sleep, thinking that this scripture can only receive a proper response by attending a Bible college or seminary. We sell the potential influence of the church short by limiting our definition of evangelism and discipleship to an institutional setting.

A family attempting to fulfill the Great Commission in the context of their own home, family, and neighborhood will most certainly come up with a configuration that challenges anything we have devised so far. Getting back to basics will include some of the following necessities:

1. Personal and "religious" behavior at home will be the rule when the church comes together. Gatherings will become celebrations of what God is doing in our personal lives and homes.

2. Personal and "religious" behavior at "church" will be the rule when the church is at home. Home life will include the same dynamics that are "enshrined" in the church services.

3. Fathers and mothers will be encouraged and taught to "train up" their own children. Professional, volunteer educators, and caregivers will be auxiliary to the discipline process rather than primary.

4. Church leaders will identify the homes of God's people as the principle sites of the church's ministry in the community. Families will be encouraged and trained to use their homes "redemptively."

5. Church leadership will discover ways to give quality time from the institutional program and schedule back to the family with guidance on how the time can best be used to disciple the family and win the neighbors.

6. Church leaders will find ways to unite the family when gathered corporately with the rest of the fellowship, rather than dividing them.

7. Disenfranchised, single, and elderly members will be invited to become parts of extended families within the fellowship.

8. A common question of leadership and heads of houses will be: "How can we better use our own homes to be the church in the community?"

BACK TO THE "THREE THOUGHTS"

Individuals and families who are able to readjust their thinking on the centrality of home and family in God's plan, as mentioned earlier, will then draw conclusions. Keep in mind that for everything to which we say "No," we are saying "Yes" to something else; and to all that we would then say "Yes," we are also saying "No" to another way or idea. Perhaps this issue of accepting more responsibility for obeying the Great Commission through the auspices of our home and family, rather than an institutional approach, will be one of the most difficult "Yes-No" decisions some of us will ever make in our entire lives. "To be honest," you are thinking, "this sounds right, but it also sounds like a huge responsibility and a lot of work!" You're right...but it's worth it!

THE COMMITMENT

Because it looks like God's heart, and it's consistent with the biblical model of New Testament church life, I intend to:

- Establish home and family as the central focus of my life. I say "No" to whatever tries to get in the way.
- Establish home and family as the principle site of Biblical discipleship in my life. I say "No" to whatever tries to keep it from happening.
- Establish home and family as the central focus of how I obey the Great Commission of Jesus. I say "No" to any other model that violates this conviction.

THE CHURCH AT HOME

It seems to me that there very well could be three levels of response to this challenge: "Household Ministries," "Home Ministries," and "House Churches." Let me give you a brief definition of each response before going any further. (See Appendix III)

Household Ministries: The response that involves mothers and fathers accepting responsibility for the spiritual training of their children.

Home Ministries: The response that involves families being willing to offer their home as a site of redemptive ministry for others.

House Churches: The response that involves places of residence being used as regular places of assembly for the church body.

"**Household Ministries**" is when one family makes up its mind that its home routine will include a regularly scheduled time when the entire family focuses its attention upon its common spiritual walk. What does God's Word have to say about it? This can be done through a "Home Night" approach or some other way that seems good to everyone, if allowed to be a high priority, that works for them as a family. (See Appendix IV)

"**Home Ministries**," modeled after the examples we find in Acts 2:42-46, 16:15, 32-34, and 28:30-31, aims at allowing your place of residence to serve as a center of redemptive life and hospitality to other individuals or families. Usually there is lot of food involved in this particular application!

Eating Together

I am impressed with the emphasis made in the Scriptures about God's people eating together. The Old Testament Passover and the New Covenant's Communion are feasts, not ceremonies. These were mere meals with profound spiritual implications. I am taken by the picture in Acts 2:46 of early believers enjoying the hospitality born out of the love God placed in our hearts for each other. This needs to be re-released in the church.

We need to have large events at the church fellowship hall, but we also need to get into each other's homes. The key to this will be hosts and hostesses getting delivered from an entertainment complex and getting back to biblical hospitality. Our culture dictates against us doing this. Restaurants, banquets, and fancy table settings crowd out simple spaghetti and popcorn balls that when done in love, with no desire to impress, turn times shared by believers in one another's homes into something so divine in its implications that it becomes almost "sacramental."

"House Churches," as you will see discussed in a later chapter in this book, is the exciting possibility of your congregation becoming a "mother church" that is involved in church planting. In this chapter, you'll see that they are more formal, in the sense that they are scheduled and are under the guidance of qualified and appointed leadership. Church members, friends, and neighbors gather in homes to worship, study, and pray. Often these groups can become the core of a new, indigenous church.

CHAPTER 5

. . . .

THE PRIORITY IS PRAISE

"Yet a time is coming and has now come when the true worshippers will worship the Father in spirit and truth, for they are the kind of worshippers the Father seeks. God is a spirit, and His worshippers must worship in spirit and in truth."

—John 4:23-24

"I F WE DO not do anything else this morning, let's be sure that we praise the Lord!" I found myself often saying this to our little congregation as we set out to become a New Testament church. The growth of the church was in direct parallel to the development of the congregation's understanding of the priority of praise. The Lord opened to our understanding a variety of Scripture passages that released us into expressions of worship that we had never known before. In this chapter we will discuss several of the principles that released a powerful sense of God's living presence in the personal as well as the corporate life of the church.

PRECEPT UPON PRECEPT

Someone has said, "Rome was not built in a day." Certainly this idea is true of everything great and enduring that has ever existed. In church building, patience is required. It takes time to see the truly great and lasting dynamics that bring sustained results.

I have learned that when something is truly important to a pastor, important enough that he or she would like to see it embraced and practiced by the congregation, then it is talked about over and over. The things we talk about the most tend to be the things that actually take root in the collective consciousness of the congregation and become a part of the corporate personality of the church.

Repetition is the backbone of education, and we must not forget that when leading people into experiencing personally our convictions as pastors. This is certainly true when it comes to bringing a congregation into a greater understanding and expression of praise.

The average church attendee is predisposed to be reserved and intimidated when it comes to public involvement in praise. In our attempts to appear sophisticated and slightly unattached, we have groomed ourselves to be careful not to give others, particularly strangers, a clue as to how we really feel about anything that involves our emotions. Our society has coached us to mask our feelings and to hide our private convictions in order to maintain decorum and protect our sensitive "parts."

I learned that simply telling people that they should praise God freely and giving a few personal examples accompanied by some "snappy" choruses was not enough – at least not enough to provoke authentic expression of their innermost beings.

THE PRIORITY IS PRAISE

We built slowly – line upon line, here a little, there a little – bringing God's people into a sense of safety to express themselves freely and without fear in praise and worship. Some of the principles that we had to learn that led us down a path to remarkable seasons of worship together were:

A. **PRAISE IS A WAY OF LIFE**
    Our concept of worship must not be limited to a particular time or place. As worshippers, we never leave the living presence of God. To perceive of worship as something that can only happen in a sanctuary or with musical accompaniment is to horribly limit our understanding of why we even exist. A church without walls looks for ways to help people become less dependent on worship accoutrements (i.e. organs, pianos, hymnals, powerpoint, leaders, etc.) and more prone to see everything they think and do as a praise offering to the Lord. The Scripture states unequivocally: *"I will bless the Lord at ALL times, His praise shall CONTINUALLY be in my mouth."*

    Worship is a moment-to-moment reality as people learn to recognize God's presence is constantly with them. Family dynamics, work habits, relational behaviors, and even hobbies suddenly become "worship services." God's people learn that they are always "having church" as far as worship is concerned.

B. **WORSHIP IS A NORMATIVE RESPONSE TO GOD'S GRACE**
    As we receive the love, forgiveness, and acceptance that blesses our relationship with God, it is only natural that praise toward God overflows from us to

Him. Worship becomes our number one priority in life. We begin to understand the psalmist's insistence on worship (i.e. *"I WILL bless the Lord."*). We begin to see why the Scriptures teach us that nature itself is inclined and poised toward praise, and that we are welcome to join all creation in the worship of our loving creator. (*"The very rocks cry out"* and *"the trees of the field clap their hands."*)

Our praise priority is not simply intellectual or obligatory. No, we worship the Lord with an awareness and joy that breeds spontaneity and deep spiritual communion. We are not just looking for a venue where we can indulge our emotions or superstitions, but rationally and with great feeling looking for scriptural avenues to vent our love to God.

SOME BASIC WAYS TO COMMUNICATE

We learned, based on these two basic convictions, that the leader needed to find a multiplicity of approaches to communicate to the congregation ways we could grow together in worship. For the first few years, that task was solely mine. As others began to understand and experience what was being taught, exhorted, and modeled, their voices began to replace my own as worship leader. If the pastor does not value praise, the people will not either. This is discipleship. I believe that it is possible, but difficult and problematic, for a congregation to grow beyond its spiritual leader in areas of primary spiritual understanding. In other words, as a pastor or leader, don't expect those who look to you for leadership to become worshippers if you are not one yourself.

PRAISE PRINCIPLES

1. God is worthy of praise.
2. We have primarily been created to praise God.
3. God inhabits the praises of His people.
4. Our greatest legacy is to leave behind another generation of praisers.
5. God must be worshipped in "spirit and in truth."

These five principles served as the "curriculum" for our pursuit of understanding and experiencing worship as a church body. Hardly a gathering would take place that one of these principles was not explored, exhorted, and practiced. Sunday to Sunday, house to house, and day to day we determined to make worship our priority.

Sometimes when we gather for one reason or another, praise is just not happening. (You can sense when worship is half-hearted or slow in presenting itself from those assembled.) We stop and talk about it. "You know," I would begin, "I don't think we are quite into it this morning. What do you think?" Many would nod their heads with a sheepish smile on their faces. "Let's give it another try," or "Let's talk about it for a few minutes."

Inevitably these items of discussion or poking fun at ourselves for holding back would precede a glorious release of heart-felt response that catapulted us into a gathering filled with the awesome sense of God's presence. We would acknowledge our humanity with no condemnation, acknowledge the worthiness of the Lord to receive our praise whether or not we "felt" like praising Him, and go on in simple obedience, which gave way to a greater sense of His blessed presence.

Never condemn or rebuke a congregation for apparent praiselessness. First, who can really see a man or woman's heart and what is actually in it? Second, people do not gather to be scolded or condemned. This type of leadership will provoke a response certainly, but what comes forth will be motivated out of guilt, not the love that prefaces true worship.

Some definitions that I have used for the terms "praise" and "worship" and the holiness that should characterize them are:

PRAISE: An expression of approval, esteem, or commendation. We praise God for who He is, not what He has done. An activity.

WORSHIP: An attitude of our innermost being directed toward God. We distinguish between praise as an act or physical expression and worship as a frame of mind… everything we do. A disposition.

EXPRESSIONS OF PRAISE

Sometimes the talent of the musicians and the charisma of the leaders can distract worshippers from the one they are worshipping (Jesus) and fix their attention on a performance. Musicians and leaders have to learn to be the means to an end (the exaltation of the Lord Jesus Christ) and not ends unto themselves.

We often referred to the congregation as "the choir," and when new songs were being introduced to the congregation we called those opportunities "choir practice." You can sense that the people appreciated being referred to and regarded as integral to the ministry team, even though they were not on a platform.

We were committed to moving away from thinking of a church service as a performance with variously talented and gifted individuals entertaining an "audience." Our biblical model constrained us to allow every member of the body to receive themselves as an integral ministering part of what was going on in the meetings. We tried not to introduce an atmosphere into our meetings that would cause people to think that what was going on there could not be reproduced in their own home or in their own personal relationships. We did not want people coming to the church building so they could worship. Our goal was that what we did called "praise" or "worship" at the gatherings was simply an overflow of what was going on normally and regularly where we lived and worked.

A WORD ABOUT ORDER

Whenever leadership encourages free and open expression, there must be scriptural guidelines that discipline or manage biblically what is going on. We search the scriptures not only for liberty, but also for Divine order. What emerged was an interesting blend of free and rather reserved people worshipping together comfortably.

How was this possible? Two reasons:

1. People were cautioned not to do anything in such a way that it would draw attention away from the Lord and to themselves. They graciously acquiesced.
2. Those gathering felt "safe" because they knew that leadership was contending for authentic praise and worship, but would never give in to inappropriate emotionalism or outbursts. If this ever happened it was handled quickly and graciously, and the opportunity was seized to teach the church about what we were searching for as a group: authentic praise and worship.

The people of God are free to express themselves from the very depths of the heart (in Spirit) and with a personal and accountable growing understanding of who the Lord is (in truth) in the following ways: (John 4:24)

1. Spoken words of adoration
2. Songs of adoration
3. Kneeling or bowing before the Lord
4. Dancing before the Lord
5. The clapping of hands in praise
6. Lifting of hands before the Lord
7. Silence before the Lord
8. Prostrating oneself before the Lord

Each of these postures of physical expressions of the heart as one involves themselves in praise has a releasing effect upon the worshipper and are biblical in their precedent. The church was released into these expressions as they were helped to understand that these were scripturally authorized ways of expressing what was in one's own heart toward the Lord. People should never be forced to conform to these ways of expressing themselves, but they should feel free to do so if they feel led.

The rule of thumb in human terms was best expressed one morning when referring to a spirit of unity prevailing in a gathering where there was a diversity of ways that people presented themselves to the Lord – some quietly, some animated, and still others somewhere in between. "Folks, the important thing for us to understand about our 'choir' of worship this morning is that there are no 'soloists.'" The congregation got the message and the meaning, and often quoted that summary when encouraging people not to use their liberty to become a license to distract or call attention to themselves in a public worship service.

GUIDELINES FOR WORSHIP LEADERS
(MUSICIANS AND SINGERS)

1. Must himself/herself be a worshipper.
2. Must know God has called him to lead others into worship.
3. Must be eager to grow in his/her knowledge of worship and why worship is so important.
4. Must be willing to become more skilled on his/her instrument.
5. Willing to be committed to loving and building up the others in the group.
6. Willing to crucify the desire to attract attention to himself/herself during worship.
7. Willing to take on the attitude of a servant. This includes following whoever is up front.
8. Must attend rehearsals and special meetings.
10. Willing to serve with a glad heart, willing to do more than what is required of him.

CHAPTER 6

DISCIPLESHIP NEEDED MORE THAN EVER

RESPONDING TO THE MANDATE

WE NEED TO take another look at the Great Commission of Jesus to His disciples found in Matthew 28:18-20:

> *"Then Jesus came to them and said, 'All authority in heaven and on earth has been given to me. Therefore go and make disciples of all nations, baptizing them in the name of the Father and of the Son and of the Holy Spirit, and teaching them to obey everything I have commanded you.'"*

I like to think of discipleship as a relational process that results in releasing ministry in another's life that is similar to your own. In other words, teaching someone to do what you do, basically the same way you do it. This process in other fields of endeavor might be referred to as an "apprenticeship" or maybe a "trial period." In ministry, to bring another along and give them the same opportunity as someone previously gave you is very "Christ like."

Today, in educational circles the term being used is "empowerment." The role of the teacher in learning is to give the student the "power" or the opportunity to discover, to choose and thereby to learn.

Each of us must choose an appropriate response to the mandate of our Lord to *"go...preach...make disciples."* Too often the choice, however, is incorrect.

Today, too many church leaders are responding to the "call" by developing an "entertainment model" of ministry. The biblical model is actually an "educational model." Let me explain the difference.

THE ENTERTAINMENT MODEL

Many spiritual leaders today seem to think of the ministry as a form of entertainment. By that I mean that their goal is applause. The standard whereby success in ministry is measured is by a "yardstick" that calibrates how well people "like" or "enjoyed" Sunday's service.

Like so many singing canaries, pastors and leaders find themselves swinging from their perch, hoping to attract some attention and hopefully do well enough that everyone will clap and come back next week. This concept of ministry success has been reinforced by the incessant emphasis on attendance figures and size of offerings. The Hollywood and Broadway criteria of a "packed-out house" is usually the way many today determine success. Unfortunately, when the goal is applause and attendance records, biblical discipleship gets lost in the cracks. The development of meaningful and accountable relationships for the purpose of spiritual maturity and personal fulfillment is forgotten and trampled in the mad rush to the ticket booth of entertainment-type spiritual leadership. Many are falling for this model of ministry today.

THE EDUCATIONAL MODEL

Spiritual leaders need to see themselves principally as educators. I am convinced that this is what Jesus had in mind when He told His disciples to *"(teach) them to obey everything I have commanded you."* To make a disciple is to move beyond attraction and assimilation into education. The criterion of successful discipleship is when life-changing learning takes place. Someone has said that the best definition of teaching is learning; and the best definition of learning is change. It seems to me that this is the goal of discipleship – men and women being *"transformed by the renewing of their mind"* – bringing them into a personal expression of the *"good, pleasing and perfect"* will of God. (Romans 12:2)

The sooner today's spiritual leaders understand and cor-rect this "slide" toward a Hollywood model of discipleship rather than a biblical model, the sooner we can rightfully assume a correct definition of the mandate to *"Go and make disciples."*

OBEDIENCE-BASED DISCIPLESHIP

Jesus said to His disciples, *"If you love me, you will obey what I command."* As we make disciples unto Jesus, we must adopt the same theme – not that people would necessarily obey us personally, but that they would learn to recognize the truth contained in God's Word and obey that.

Jesus clearly claims the church as His. In Matthew 16:18, He states that it is HIS church, and HE will build it. He gave His disciples only a handful of direct commands that He expected to be obeyed. He expects the same from His modern-day disciples as well. A careful study of the four Gospels reveals that while Jesus taught and modeled much, surprisingly He only gave His disciples a "short list" of absolutes that He expected obeyed if His blessing was to be realized.

The Commands of Christ

1. Luke 24:49: *"Stay in the city until you have been clothed with power from on high."*
2. Luke 14:26-27: *"anyone who does not carry his cross and follow me, cannot be my disciple."*
3. John 4:23-24: *"God is spirit, and His worshippers MUST worship Him in spirit and truth."*
4. John 13:34-35: *"A new commandment I give you: Love one another."*
5. Matthew 24:42: *"Therefore keep watch, because you do not know on which day your Lord will return."*
6. Matthew 28:18-20: *"Go…make disciples."*

I end this list and chapter where I began – with the words of our Lord Jesus, the master disciple-maker. They come ringing down through the corridors of history, calling us to an obedience-based concept of ministry, resulting in the release of ministry accountable to the many lives we touch. We are not to "use" people to accomplish our goals and agenda. As leaders we have been told to "develop" people into all they can be in Jesus.

RELEASING RELIABLE MINISTRY

Paul admonished his son in the faith in 2 Timothy 2:2: *"entrust to reliable men who will also be qualified to teach others."* Important words in this charge to be understood are: "entrust," "reliable," and qualified." Proceeding with the application of this mandate for discipleship without serious thought to the ramifications of trust, reliability and qualification with regard to those being released into leadership could be absolutely disastrous.

The key to an orderly release of spiritual authority in a church body is healthy and accountable relationships. If this factor is overlooked for the sake of convenience or impatience, it will almost always result in a breakdown or a break-up down the line somewhere. Most problems can be avoided when leadership takes the time to get to know people well before giving them a job, a title, or a position. When there is a free exchange of ideas, backgrounds, philosophies, and plans, a foundation of a long-term working relationship can be laid. Trust is built and character is confirmed. The process involved effectively qualifies those involved for reliable ministry.

For me, three words summarize the responsibility of a pastor or the leader of any spiritually oriented group or organization as far as their responsibility to develop and delegate leadership is concerned: **recognize**, **cultivate**, and **release**. These words succinctly describe the stages of a relationship that a leader should have with those he or she desires to release into ministry. As these stages are conscientiously observed, the result is the kind of reliable and qualified leadership the church needs and deserves.

It is easier to gloss over these stages of relationship in a headlong pursuit of program goals. However, disregarding the checks and balances that are provided us through carefully developed personal relationships will result in hurtful disillusionments and misconceptions.

A. Recognize

A leader should be neither threatened nor "taken in" by talent or charm. A sparkling personality, charming mannerisms, striking appearance, or even Bible knowledge do not make a leader. Nothing can take the place of the unmistakable, pure anointing of the Holy Spirit on a man or woman's life. Leaders need to look for the anointing in the lives of those they lead. You might ask, "What does the anointing look like?" From my years of sometimes guessing, other times manipulating, and lots of times making trouble for myself, I have finally come to realize what it is I am looking for when I am "looking for the anointing."

1. Look for someone whom others are following. The best definition of a leader I ever heard is simply: a leader is someone who is being followed. A sure indicator of God's leadership grace in a life is when God is obviously giving them favor with the people of God. This "Principle of Ascendancy" has proven to be a built-in safeguard for me in spotting those the Lord wants to use.

2. Look for someone who is not interested in fame or power. Jesus made it very clear that those who were going to be His disciples would have to settle the "Gentile" or secular issues of coercive power. He could only use servants – selfless people who were not seeking responsibility or position for the sake of "lording it" over others. The same goes for today, particularly in light of the very unhealthy ideas people have about authority and authority figures.

3. Look for a leader whose "house is in order." The best gauge for anointing that I know is the countenance of the one in question's spouse. If they are not married, then you will have to take a look at their relationship with their parents (regardless of their age). If they are a parent, then look for obedient children. No single qualification for leadership

stated in the New Testament is more emphasized than the way one "rules" his house. This stands to reason when you consider the biblical injunctions that present the church as a family. Leadership has to work at home first.

While this list could probably go on, these are the "vital signs." Every time I have compromised the list, I was sorry later and regretted my impatience. Look for the visible and obvious fruit of the Holy Spirit's presence in the life. If it isn't obvious to all concerned, then wait. I believe this is what the Scriptures are saying to us when they state emphatically: *"do not be hasty in the laying on of hands"* (1 Timothy 5:22).

B. Cultivate

Remember, according to Ephesians 4:12 a pastor *"prepares God's people for work of service."* A spiritual leader should be dedicated to the development of God's grace in people's lives. Every leader who wants to see discipleship take place must have some kind of a "cultivation plan" in mind – a strategy to train and develop those the Lord sends you for ministry. Some of the keys for the cultivation of leadership are:

1. Be willing to spend time informally with those you are working with. This is not just a "classroom-type" relationship.
2. Determine and prioritize the principles and issues that you feel are a "must" for the developing leader to understand from you and focus your attention on these.
3. Observe the "vital signs" and talk about them:

a. Submission to authority
b. Servant attitude about ministry
c. Family life
d. Integrity and reliability

First Timothy 3 is a wonderful criterion for the "cultivation plan" of any leader involved in discipling new leaders. This section of Scripture gives me the agenda that I need to help my brothers and sisters become the "overseers" that their hearts are set to be (1 Timothy 3:1).

C. Release

This is the most difficult stage of the relationship. Everything is on the line now and certain risks are involved. It is time to let go of the one you have found, built a relationship with, and trained. Such is the nature of the role of a leader. We live in a world that could be likened to a "revolving door" because of our responsibility to first recognize God's grace in a life, then to draw close and assist in the cultivation of that grace, and finally to let them go out on their own.

God has given each of us a chance to prove ourselves in ministry. As leaders, we should be willing to do the same for those we train. We will never know for sure how well we have done until we release them.

Control says, "They will fail without me," or "I can do it better." Release says, "Give them a chance," or "Maybe they will do it better than me."

The releasing leader is one who understands Jesus' heart when He taught His disciples to "go." The greatest crown of accomplishment any spiritual leader could ever wear would be when someone they recognized, cultivated, and released experienced even more fruitfulness in ministry than they had personally ever known.

Share the load, share the vision, and share the glory. Make disciples, build men and women – it is one of life's greatest thrills!

CHAPTER 7

. . . .

SPIRITUAL REPRODUCTION

PERHAPS NOTHING IN the human experience equals the joy, as well as the agony, that we experience in the drama of childbirth and parenthood.

Strangely, a growing number of married couples elect to "pass" when it comes to adding another life to their family. The reasons vary. Some are frightened by the prospects of raising children in the kind of world they see developing around them. Others find that paranoia erupts in their minds whenever they begin to consider the stress and pain of pregnancy and the birth process. Still others simply do not want parental responsibilities and inconveniences to "clutter up" their carefully planned life agendas.

These kinds of attitudes present a startling and very troubling counterpoint to the many couples that tragically find themselves barren – biologically incapable of life's greatest and most fulfilling miracle. For these, reproduction eludes them; for the others, reproduction is terrifying, unwanted, or untimely.

Of course, we can't consider this subject for very long before the horror of abortion and the nightmare of infanticide enter to suggest an even greater disintegration of our culture's value of life and its celebration of birth.

"WE'RE GOING TO HAVE A BABY!"

Because this concept of "spiritual reproduction" was understood by a majority of our congregation, time and time again this announcement was made: "We're going to have a baby!" The commitment to plant churches was with us from the very beginning, but the actual way in which it was done evolved over a period of time. Appendix VI contains the philosophy and procedures that resulted in the successful planting of over a dozen congregations involving hundreds of people. Be sure to read the appendix entitled "A Biblical Pattern for Church Growth" if you are interested in how to release a congregation into becoming a "mother church."

It is into this nomenclature of human biological reproduction with all of its "swirl" of issues and attitudes today that I choose to dramatize my approach to the subject of church planting for our times – in the twenty-first century.

Today, a term has been coined to describe the wonder of birth, and the fact that we can reproduce ourselves at all is "the sanctity of life." In a few words, we celebrate what God has set in motion and remind ourselves of a basic value that, if lost, threatens our very civilization.

It seems to me that all of these same attitudes, issues, and values actually exist when it comes to the subject of church planting, as planting a church is very much like having a baby.

THE LAW OF SPIRITUAL REPRODUCTION

Several years ago I developed a concept of discipleship that ultimately leads to a mandate for church planting. I proposed that since Genesis Chapter One, we have been charged with a mandate *"to be fruitful and multiply."* As New Testament believers, we are given another mandate or Great Commission by our Lord Jesus to *"make disciples."* Paul reminded his spiritual son Timothy to *"commit thou to faithful men who in turn will teach others also."* These dynamic orders, along with many other references to and examples of discipleship found throughout the Scriptures, clearly teach us that the mission to reproduce ourselves spiritually is our most appropriate response to the Gospel. To most of my readers, what I have just summarized is nothing particularly new. I do propose that most of us do not easily or readily identify with a "spiritual reproduction" model for our lives, nor do we basically prescribe as individuals or as groups to what I call "The Law of Spiritual Reproduction."

It is very simple, "Anything healthy is reproducible." As you can see, I have taken it from a basic law of nature, but it beautifully applies itself to the church.

With all of this in mind, may I now ask you a question? Would you like to have a baby? The question appropriately fits the New Testament metaphor of the church being like a human body. Read 1 Corinthians 12:12-27 and Ephesians 4:15-17. All of the drama and the trauma that we associate with childbearing and childbirth are present when one or more sets out to plant a church – to reproduce.

Would you like to have a baby? A baby church that is a small microcosm of whatever your local church has become by the grace of God. Remember the law? "Anything healthy is reproducible." It calls out, demanding a response from what until now has been a largely indifferent constituency– a possible body of spiritual parents that is staggering in its potential when you begin to think about it; but who seem to be plagued with some of the same attitudes and polarized by many of the same issues I summarized earlier. However, now the issues are in fact spiritual, not biological or moral.

Again, pastor, church member, I present you with the question: Would you like to have a baby? I think you are beginning to understand what I'm asking you. Or, excuse me, but are you afraid, pre-occupied, or (perish the thought) not healthy enough?

Now don't get defensive on me. Let's be friends. We are all struggling with issues of obedience to God's Word. This is but one issue, and certainly not the most important one at that, but for some of us it does center on where the Lord is dealing with us at this time. Acknowledge the abundance of His grace in our churches and become willing, excited in fact, to reproduce it somewhere else.

SOME THINGS TO CONSIDER

Before we go any further, let's count the costs:

1. There is pain involved in having a baby.
2. It's always better to plan for a baby's arrival.
3. It costs money to have a baby.
4. Making a baby is one thing; raising a baby is another.
5. Babies usually do best in the hands of mature yet vigorous parents.
6. Sometimes it's not a good idea to have lots of babies.

Probably it is a good idea to consider the benefits as well:

1. There is joy involved in having a baby.
2. There is great fulfillment in having a baby.

3. Childbirth is one of life's greatest character developers.
4. Healthy babies become healthy adults.

RULES OF CONCEPTION

There are three prerequisites for responsible conception of life:

A. Health (The physical ability to conceive)
B. Passion (The love it takes to share)
C. Covenant (The commitment to care)

A couple, if pregnant without all three of these prerequisites, is in trouble; and that certainly goes for their child as well. The congregation that embarks on a "mothering" vision must have these qualities established firmly within the "body-life" of the believers. **Health:** a modicum of assets that is available spiritually and physically. **Passion:** motivated by genuine compassion for unreached people, and a care for each other. **Covenant:** Responsible, mature commitment to the process and whatever it may bring. (Remember, birth does have its surprises!) So, do you want to have a baby?

HOW TO HAVE A BABY (CHURCH...THAT IS)

1. ENCOURAGE A GROWTH ATTITUDE AMONG THE BELIEVERS
   The natural consequence of health is growth, and in its maturity, reproduction. Let this always be the goal. The key ingredient that motivates growth is love. (John 3:16, 13:35) Compassion for the lost and obedience to the great commission must characterize the attitude of a mature congregation that wants to be a reproducing body.

2. DEVELOP MATURE SPIRITUAL LEADERSHIP
    Ephesians 4:11-12 teaches us that the primary
    work of church leaders is to build up the people of
    God and prepare them for the work of the ministry.
    Discipleship will produce strong bodies, and strong
    bodies will produce prepared leaders to become the
    catalysts of new works.

3. DEVELOP A PLAN OR STRATEGY FOR GROWTH
    AND REPRODUCTION
    "Those who fail to plan, plan to fail." Jesus taught
    His disciples to "count the costs" before they set out
    to follow His teaching. The local church looking
    to grow and reproduce needs a non-manipulated,
    Spirit-directed plan born in the Word and confirmed
    through prayer and fasting.

4. LOOK FOR RIPE AND RECEPTIVE COMMUNITIES
    OF PEOPLE
    Careful awareness of what is going on around us
    will help us to note trends and changes that might
    possibly open doors to fruitful harvest. The parable
    of the sower is interpreted by Jesus in Matthew
    13:18-23. In His explanation, we learn that in our
    societies some are resistant while at the same time
    others are receptive to the Gospel by following
    Christians who move from one community to
    another or by going with new converts back to their
    families and friends.

5. DEVELOP HOME GROUPS IN FERTILE FIELDS
    Fifty years ago a storefront or a tent was the way in
    which church planting was accomplished. Today, it

is the residences of believers. It is a Biblical model. (Acts 5:42, 20:20) In this environment the Christian faith is both taught and modeled in a non-threatening atmosphere. Home groups, properly led, become indigenous churches. The church planter's home, when properly ordered as a refuge for his or her family and a place of hospitality for the community, will emanate life from this warm and peaceful family setting.

6. SEEK OUT "NORMAL" RELATIONSHIPS
   Pursue avenues of communication and social contact with members of the community through secular channels, schools, clubs, sports organizations, business community, etc. From this, you will develop Spirit-led contacts that will lead to ministry opportunities. Involve every member of your family in this kind of initial outreach. Open your home to these people.

7. NETWORK WITH THE PARA-CHURCH ORGANIZATIONS
   Cultivate good relationships with existing ministries if they exist in the area of your effort. Become involved in these evangelistic outreaches and benevolent programs. Become a follow-up resource for Christian broadcast ministries.

8. BEGIN A WEEKLY BIBLE STUDY IN YOUR HOME
   It was natural for the early Christians to open their homes to gather for worship, fellowship, and teaching. (Romans 16:5; 1 Corinthians 16:19; Colossians 4:15) Invite your contacts to attend, advertise

the meeting if permissible, and keep the subject material basic. This will lead to the organization of a church body.

CHAPTER 8

· ·

WORLD CHRISTIANS

SOME WERE SCATTERED and the others were sent. In Jerusalem, the expansion and extension of the church was forced by external influences beyond their control. Later in Antioch, things seemed well planned and sequential. The continued outward expansion of the church from this key Gentile city goes forward with the precision of internal strategy. (Read Acts 13:13)

THE NEW TESTAMENT MODEL
OF MISSIONS

A look at the early church is incomplete without zooming in on the way they responded to Jesus' Great Commission. The "table of contents" of the book of Acts has to be found in chapter one, verse eight: *"But you will receive power when the Holy Spirit comes on you; and you will be my witnesses in Jerusalem"* (1:1-8:3) *and in all Judea and Samaria* (8:4-12:25) *and to the ends of the earth"* (13:1-28:31).

Bringing a congregation, especially an affluent one, into a proper response to the Great Commission is a challenge. In this chapter, I would like to share with you how the Holy Spirit averted our growing church from falling into the abyss of "Country Club Christianity."

WORLD CHRISTIANITY

I had never heard the term "World Christians" until I read the book *On the Crest of the Wave* by B. Peter Wagner (Regal Books). His appeal for a more authentic response to the incredible needs world-wide agreed with the growing convictions that were spiraling up inside my own heart for our congregation of mostly affluent people to become more involved in the obvious needs in less comfortable neighborhoods of our county, as well as various parts of the entire world.

While the vast majority of our growing churches were deeply dedicated people, and all gave testimony of a personal relationship with Jesus Christ, very few indicated even the slightest interest in cross-cultural ministry. The financial giving was growing constantly, but only a fraction of it was ever designated for "missions." Comparatively, small interest seemed to be shown toward any kind of an effort or program that had to do with missionaries or missions.

Was this a sign of unspirituality? Was this an indication of some deep-sealed prejudice or bigotry? Or, did this lack of interest in responding to Jesus' heart for the world mean that we were yet another comfortable North American congregation needing to be stirred from our typically naïve perspective of the globe? That perspective could be described as ethnocentricity, myopic, and shortsighted.

SOMETHING BEGAN TO HAPPEN

Every year we welcomed the ministry of a man of God, who our congregation received as an important "voice" to our congregation. His ministry was generally regarded by our leadership and by the congregation as an expression of the Ephesians 4:11 "prophet." On this particular Sunday morning visit, he shared with us a passage of Scripture that he believed the Lord had given to him as a directive for our church's immediate future, as far as our outreach into the community and world was concerned. The passage is found in 2 Chronicles 28:14-15:

> *"So the soldiers gave up the prisoners and the plunder in the presence of the officials and all the assembly. The men designated by name took the prisoners and from the plunder they clothed all who were naked. They provided them with clothes and sandals, food and drink, and healing balm. All those who were weak they put on donkeys. So they took them back to their fellow countrymen."*

These verses have to do with the aftermath of a battle between the two Jewish kingdoms of Israel and Judah. Judah languished under the morally and spiritually bankrupt leadership of King Ahaz. In one day, the warriors of Samaria and their commander-king, Pekah, had slaughtered 120,000 of Judah's soldiers. The Scriptures clearly state that the defeat was the direct consequence of Judah's refusal to obey the commands of the Lord.

What is interesting here is the uncharacteristically kind and gentle treatment on behalf of the Samaritans toward the prisoners of war from Jerusalem. The prophet Oded had warned the Samaritans that the Lord required them to return the prisoners or there would be fearsome consequences.

A principle of mercy toward those who have suffered either unduly or because of their disobedience emerges here. Too often we decide whether or not an individual, a community, or a nation deserve our Christian benevolence, prayers, and attention. Usually, we are introducing into that unilateral decision a whole agenda of personal biases.

This story from Israeli history illustrates for us the point that wherever there is suffering, regardless of the reason – even God's judgment – the godly response is benevolent and immediate action. We do not have the right to decide whether God loves a people group or an individual – He simply does. He loves us all the same.

THE CHALLENGE

The challenge that came to us that day so forcefully from our prophet-guest was to get involved in loving all humanity the way God does. We were challenged to allow the Lord to give us a heart large enough to accommodate the whole world. In my way of thinking, that is the definition of what it means to be a "World Christian."

While they might help, no amount of missions conferences, missionary guests, trips to foreign countries, or book reports can take the place of one individual opening his heart wide to the world in a prayer of repentance for being self-consumed to the point of utter unconcern or disdain for a world full of alcoholism, sex perversion, HIV virus, child abuse, homelessness, hunger, occultism, paganism, and ignorance.

It was time for all of us to become "World Christians."

NO ROOM IN THE INN

The following is the abridged text of a Christmas Eve sermon I felt directed to bring to the church in response to the challenge to take the "plunder" of God's blessings in our lives and use it to minister to the world's prisoners of circumstance far less comfortable than our own. The message brought a response that resulted in our church finding its more correct and "Christian" place among the prisoners of our society and our world.

Bethlehem was crowded. Hundreds had come from throughout the land to register for the census and pay their taxes. The normally quiet little village a few miles outside Jerusalem was filled with the hustle and bustle of inconvenienced yet law-abiding citizens, who had come to do their business as quickly as possible and then get out of the little "God-forsaken" town. Bethlehem was one of those kinds of places that it is nice to be from!

The inn was full. There was probably only one in town, and it would have been small and simple. On the other hand, it would also be clean and warm – a sparse but welcome refuge from the stinging cold of a Judean wilderness night.

When Joseph inquired, he was probably not surprised that there was no room. After all, a Nazarene carpenter would not have had a slave to run ahead and make a reservation request. And you could be sure that others would have been able to pay a better price for the rooms so greatly in demand than he. You see, it was a "dog-eat-dog" world then too. You might think that a pregnant girl grimacing in the pains of labor would have gotten them a room out of sheer sympathy – don't believe it. Roman Judea wasn't that kind of a world any more than the jostled streets and parking lots of our region today.

It was strictly the survival of the fittest. The rich were getting richer and the poor were getting poorer. Mary and Joseph were numbered among the poorest of the poor. Their Nazareth address was a stigma over their heads like a drab cloud as they moved slowly down the Bethlehem road: "Can anything good come out of Nazareth?"

Did the inn have a name? It seems that establishments of that type might. "Shalom House" or maybe "Bartholomew's Place" or whatever – we don't know.

Today, I would like to give that inn a name. Let's call it "Fame and Fortune." And like Joseph's predicament, the place seems to always be filled – unavailable at those times when you really need a room the most. Very few people ever make it to the "top" in this world. Some are injured, some are discouraged, some are ill advised, and others are simply too far out of reach.

But even if all were able to get to the "top," it seems there is little room there. The space is in much demand and many crowd around, hoping to occupy the precious space called "Fame and Fortune." There are so many applicants for the best jobs and the best schools, the best houses and the best clubs, and prices so high for the best clothing and the best food – there just isn't room.

This Christmas morning I am aware that most of those to whom I speak have made it to the inn called "Fame and Fortune." That's right; we represent the "in crowd." We have a room, we planned ahead, we worked hard, and some of us were even "given a break." We are at the top of our field or getting there fast.

"Thank God!" "Praise the Lord!" "Hallelujah!"

We are very grateful, and there is nothing to be ashamed of. There is nothing wrong with having a room in the inn. But we must remember something very important, if we are going to remember anything at all about what Christmas means, there is another place where there is room for everyone. This place is called the manger. It is small, it is dirty and stinks of "animals," but it is the place where the Son of God, the King of kings was born; and there is always enough room there for everybody.

Now, not many people are jostling to get in there. But if we really love people and care about them, we will do everything we can to tell them how to "get in out of the cold." There are approximately three million people in America who are homeless tonight. You say, "Yeah, but they are mentally ill, alcoholic, or criminally inclined." That may be true of some of them, but don't forget – they are people. Each and every one is an individual drama, a life that Jesus died for and that He cares about. If we add the two million homeless in Europe, the ten million homeless in the Third World, the 225,000 politically disposed in Central America, and another 900,000 wanderers in Africa, we are up to a staggering total.

Excuse me for spoiling your shopping sprees, but twenty-three percent of the United States population lives below the official poverty line of this land: $9,862.00 per year for a family of four (1988).

There is no room in the inn called "Fame and Fortune," and frankly, I wonder if mature Christians should even try to get in. There is, however, room in the manger.

> But I, the Messiah, shall come in my glory, and all the angels with me. And I will separate the people as a shepherd separates the sheep from the goats, and place the sheep at my right hand, the goats at my left. Then I, the King, shall say to those on my right, "Come, blessed of my Father, into the kingdom prepared for you from the founding of the world. For I was hungry and you fed me; I was thirsty and you gave me water; I was a stranger and you invited me into your homes; naked and you clothed me; sick and in prison and you visited me."

Then these righteous ones shall reply, "Sir, when did we ever see you hungry and feed you, or thirsty and give you anything to drink? Or a stranger, and helped you? Or naked, and clothe you? When did we ever see you sick or in prison and visit you?" And I, the King, will tell them, "When you did it to these brothers, you were doing it to me!" Then I will turn to those on my left and say, "Away with you, you cursed ones, into eternal fire prepared for the devil and his demons. For I was hungry, and you would not feed me; thirsty, and you would not give me anything to drink; a stranger, and you refused me hospitality; naked, and you would not clothe me; sick and in prison, and you did not visit me." Then they will reply, "Lord, when did we ever see you hungry or thirsty or a stranger or naked or sick or in prison, and not help you?" And I will answer, "When you refused to help the least of these my brothers, you were refusing to help me." And they shall go away into eternal punishment, but the righteous into everlasting life.
—Matthew 25:31-46

Over the past several months, I have been dragged – kicking and screaming – by the hand of the Lord into a new assessment of my understanding of what constitutes a true Christian response to my society's and world's needs. James 1:27 states, *"Religion that God our Father accepts as pure and faultless is this: to look after orphans and widows in their distress, and to keep oneself from being polluted by the world."*

What I share now is intensely personal and offered as one man's plight to find the "manger" – discover where true Christianity really takes an individual. "I am not my own, I have been bought with a price." That is what the Scripture says about me or anyone else, for that matter, who luxuriates in the personal knowledge of the forgiveness of their sins.

Through a painful process, I have recently been reduced to the common denominator of being simply only a product of the grace and mercy of God. I have been systematically, yet lovingly stripped of all pretenses and made to know: *"for me to live is Christ, but to die is gain."* The experience I speak of is still new and incomplete, and far too personal and subjective to be able to explain. Nevertheless, it has taken place in your own life. Others of you, because you love and trust me and follow me, will come to grips with this matter. Still others will be frightened away by the implications.

I have been forced to look upon my selfish definition of Christian discipleship. One that, among other things, takes far too light of an attitude towards sin and far too indifferent an attitude towards the weak, poor, and ill of this planet.

I have been reminded that even though we have much to be thankful for today and reason to rejoice in the Lord's faithfulness and blessings, we must look around. Our life-styles are of such a nature that fewer than twenty percent of the people in our own country are able to live like most of us do. Our country is a member of a rare "club" within earth's population. We represent a rather insignificant percentage of the total population; yet, with the rest of the industrialized nations, consume eighty percent of the world's products. I have shut most of the world out of my mind. There has been no room for them in my concept of the "inn." But now I'm looking with renewed commitment at the "manger."

Since my eyes have been opened lately, I find Jesus in humble places – away from the glitzy and glamour of evangelical, charismatic-type Christianity. I see Him in "mangers" among the poor and disposed, being humble, like a child, being a servant – willing to inhabit stable-like places where things smell and "animals" are present. In other words, where there is room for everyone.

Jesus says, *"Come unto me all that labor and are heavy laden and I will give you rest."* I want to be sure that my life echoes that kind of compassion to everyone:

- Regardless of race
- In spite of their background
- Whatever their disease
- No matter where they live
- Even if they doubt my intentions

When we think of the hurt in people's lives today, it is no longer acceptable for it to be more demanding to form a commitment to be a member of the Lions Club (for example) than it is to be a member of the church of Jesus Christ. I believe that we stand at a crossroads in the path of our life as a church family. I believe the year ahead of us will "tell the tale" as to whether or not God can use us to really make a difference in our world.

Two weeks ago, a prophet stood in our midst and gave our fellowship a word from 2 Chronicles 28:15. The passage speaks of the compassionate behavior of a victorious army of fighting men, who after defeating their enemy tenderly provided for their now-vanquished adversaries with clothes, shoes, food, drink, and healing. They gave them transportation and safe passage back home. In short, they gave them restoration. I believe that this is a picture of our destiny as far as outreach is concerned. We should be a people who defeats kings and thrones of Hell through spiritual warfare, and then gently, practically, restore those who were enslaved to everything that had been taken from them. Not "hand-outs" or just missionary offerings. We want to offer in Jesus' name spiritual deliverance and practical assistance.

This is dirty work. It takes place often in stable-like places. We must go to the cities, the farms, the streets, the prisons, the hospitals, and the nations. We must break away from only thinking about ourselves. The Tri-Valley area is our parish – it is where we live safely, warmly, comfortably.

We concentrate much of our efforts here, but there is much more waiting for us beyond this valley's green hills.

CHAPTER 9

THE CHURCH CHRIST RETURNS FOR

"In my Father's house are many rooms; if it were not so, I would have told you. I am going there to prepare a place for you. And if I go and prepare a place for you, I WILL COME BACK and take you to be with me that you also may be where I am."

—John 14:2-3

"For as the lightning comes from the east and flashes to the west, so will be the coming of the Son of Man...Therefore keep watch, because you do not know the day or the hour."
—Matthew 24:27 and 25:13

LIVING ON THE EDGE OF TIME

ALL OF MY life I have lived with the belief that Jesus would be returning soon. I first heard it preached as a very small boy. The imminence of Jesus' return was an important factor in the commitment of my life to His Lordship as a young teenager. And then, I found myself preaching sermons of my own that sounded very much like the ones I had heard as a boy. Life goes on – the church continues to march through history towards her vague but certain destiny as the "Bride of Christ" and the "Marriage Supper of the Lamb."

I don't happen to be a student of biblical prophecies concerning the second coming of the Lord Jesus. I fervently believe, however, in His literal-physical return for His own. Among other passages on the subject, Matthew 24 and 25 loom large in my mind as important guidelines for every believer's attitude and behavior on the subject of Christ's return.

It seems to me that we are sitting on the very edge of time as we have entered into the twenty-first century. Jesus had quite a lot to say in response to His disciple's question in Matthew 24:3: *"Tell us,"* they said, *"when will this happen, and what will be the sign of your coming and of the end of the age?"* His response is recorded in the remainder of the chapter, and then He shares three parables in chapter 25 that help us understand the manner in which our Lord would have us live if we really believe He is coming back.

THREE PARABLES FOR "WATCHERS"

For those who are trying to follow the admonition of Matthew 24:42 (*"Therefore keep watch"*), the parables of the "Ten Virgins" (25:1-13), the "Talents" (25:14-30), and the "Sheep and the Goats" (25:31-46) are encouraging. The "Ten Virgins" remind us that we are to remain in a constant state of anticipation and personal preparedness for the Lord's return. The parable of the "Talents" is a striking challenge to be actively involved in God's redemptive plan as we await His return. For each of us, there is a strategic role to play in the meantime. We must not be idle in our waiting. The parable of the "Sheep and the Goats" addresses what may be the most critical issue to face the church awaiting Christ's return today. The alleviation of real human suffering through practical and conscientious ministry is the cry of the hour. Jesus is coming back, yes! It may be today or tomorrow, or still years from now. The church is challenged by Jesus to give itself away in compassion and abandon to the massive needs and sores that exist in our times – the "last times."

A church that is anticipating Christ's return, activating herself to participation in redeeming the lost, and committed to practically alleviating the crying needs of people is for sure living on the "edge of time."

THE CHURCH AND HIS RETURN

I believe that Jesus is returning for a church like the church He left here on earth. The beautiful passage in Ephesians 5:22-33 that the writer refers to as *"a profound mystery…about Christ and the church"* (verse 29) in my opinion speaks strongly to the condition of the church at the time of the return of Jesus as He has promised.

When speaking of the goal of a husband in his ministry to his own wife, verse 27 states: *"to make her holy cleansing her by the washing with water through the Word, and to present her to himself as a radiant church without stain or wrinkle or any other blemish, but holy and blameless"* (Ephesians 5:26-27). This is the goal of our Lord Jesus for His bride, His church. This is what the church will look like when Jesus comes back for her. Jesus is coming back for a church like the one He left!

He is returning for a "radiant church," without stain or wrinkle or any other blemish, but "holy and blameless." These words, to say the least, are intimidating. In fact, some English versions of the Bible refer to the church in this verse as a "perfect church." We all know that there isn't one of those around! So, where does that leave us? Let's take a look at the words that construct this important verse:

EPHESIANS 5:27
"radiant"
"without sin"
"without wrinkle"
"without blemish"
"holy"
"blameless"

This collection of words and phrases describes the church for which Jesus is returning. What do they mean? Is it possible? What is the church of Jesus supposed to look like at the end of the age? The church that Jesus is coming for is a church like the church we read about in the Acts of the Apostles – a vivacious, beautiful, youthful bride. A young church...an "early" church.

If we really believe that Jesus could come back at any time, even in our lifetime, then that conviction must have an effect upon the way we live our lives. What can we do? Live like He is returning today. I am not saying that we become frenzied or panic-stricken. I am saying that we stop living in a "business as usual" attitude when it comes to the things of God; but that we live every day as an adventure, anticipating that this day may be the day of our Lord's return for a church that is radiant and ready!

CHAPTER 10

. . . .
A FINAL PLEA FOR SIMPLICITY

MOST OF US are not capable of recreating the wheel even though we try. It seems to me that we would be better off simply applying biblical examples as we see them at face value rather than trying to improve upon them. For example, how many direct commands did Jesus give His disciples? There must have been hundreds. Church polity today definitely leaves one with the general impression that Jesus, the Lord of the church, had a lot to say about how we should "run His business."

Some time ago, I read the four Gospels with the above question uppermost in my mind. Now, I am not a Bible scholar by any stretch of the imagination, but I can read. I was surprised to find that while Jesus taught many lessons, performed many miracles, and had many conversations, He did not give His disciples many direct commands. In other words, "Fellas, this is something you must do, if you're going to be one of my disciples" (Luke 14:26-27, paraphrase).

As I read, I prepared to compile a list as long as my arm; but when I finished the exercise I was amazed to find only the following direct commands from Jesus to His disciples:

COMMAND: BE ENDUED WITH POWER!

Luke 24:29   *"I am going to send you what my Father has promised; but stay in the city until you have been clothed with power from on high."*

COMMAND: I MUST BE FIRST IN YOUR LIFE!

Luke: 14:26-27   *"If anyone comes to me and does not hate his father and mother, his wife and children, his bothers and sisters - yes even his own life - he cannot be my disciple. And anyone who does not carry his cross and follow me cannot be my disciple."*

COMMAND: WORSHIP GOD FROM YOUR HEART

John 4:24   *"God is spirit, and His worshippers must worship in spirit and in truth."*

COMMAND: LOVE ONE ANOTHER!

John 13:34   *"A new commandment I give you: Love one another. As I have loved you, so you must love one another."*

COMMAND: WATCH FOR MY RETURN!

Matthew 24:42   *"Therefore keep watch, because you
                 do not know on what day your Lord
                 will come."*

COMMAND: PREACH THE GOSPEL AND
                MAKE DISCIPLES!

Matthew 28:19-20 *"Therefore go and make disciples
                  of all nations, baptizing them in the
                  name of the Father and of the Son
                  and of the Holy Spirit, and teaching
                  them to obey everything that I have
                  commanded you."*

Now this might seem like an oversimplification to you, but your own study will not come up with many more. I don't claim that this list is absolutely complete, but it makes my point. What Jesus had in mind when He put his church together and what it has evolved into over the past two millennia are not the same. His idea was far more profound, but it looked far simpler.

As leaders and members of the church of Jesus Christ today, we would do better to keep it simple. To concentrate on effectively communicating and living the few things Jesus gave us to do, rather than compromising and dissipating our effectiveness by adding to our mission and to our message content and activity that have nothing to do with the original commission.

BURN THE SUGGESTION BOX

Let's burn our suggestion boxes and get out our Bibles. Let's cancel a few committee meetings and go to our knees, asking the Lord to show us what His church is supposed to look like in our town or city. By keeping things simple and obeying the commands of the "Head of the church," we can then find excellence in doing a few things well, rather than in the trap of spreading ourselves too thin, competing with the world's program, and allowing our cultural expectations to define our churches rather than the way it's supposed to be – the church defining the culture and its norms of behavior.

CHURCH AND CULTURE

Somewhere along the line, the church as a whole stopped talking to the world it lived in and became content talking to itself. The picture I get is that of a dog chasing its own tail. In Matthew chapter 5, Jesus speaks of people who bless the nations with brilliance and a seasoning that is persistent and unmistakable. This is a church that shapes its culture and sets the pace.

I call this "viability." Remember, a congregation attains viable status in their community when the way they are as a group has a very real effect upon the way life is lived in their wider community. Their prayers, their behavior, their credibility – these factors and others – bring lasting impact upon the way a community operates. The schools, the marketplace, the government, and the neighborhoods – all of these and more – take on a certain symmetry because God's people are there.

Now, I am not talking about the church becoming issue oriented. There is a time for placards and marches, but viability is a way of life, not an isolated demonstration. It is the life of Jesus Christ being lived out so authentically in our own homes that people take note. It is the power of the Holy Spirit being ministered so credibly that individual lives are simply changed. It is the Kingdom of God coming in practicality as men, women, boys, and girls shape their culture in Jesus' name, rather than their culture telling them what the church is to do and be. I believe this is what Jesus had in mind when He told His disciples: *"And I tell you that you are Peter, and on this rock I will build my church, and the gates of Hades will not overcome it"* (Matthew 16:18).

FORMULATING A SIMPLIFIED PHILOSOPHY OF MINISTRY

Bringing a congregation into the simplicity of ministry that releases genuine power and authority is not as easy as it might seem. Human nature has a propensity to want to complicate matters whenever possible. As Christians, we have a subconscious need to try to atone for our sins. Consequently, we tend to add works to our service for God to appease our self-doubts. All of this adds up to bulky programs, complex doctrines, and busy schedules. The need to please is strong as well. Well-meaning people often have a suggestion or an idea that they honestly think may be the very thing that will "spark" a revival or get more people involved in the church program. We all have our "pet projects" and proven "whiz bang" programs that worked somewhere else and seem to be "worth a try." The busy leader, sometimes grasping for straws, is constantly tempted to implement just about anything that might work, or at least keep people off his or her back. This is not the way to go about developing a philosophy of ministry.

WHERE TO START

It is always good to start at the beginning. The beginning needs to be a set of basic and fundamental questions. May I suggest the following:

1. What is your ultimate goal(s) or dream in ministry?
2. What does the Word of God have to say about your goal(s)?
3. How do you plan to accomplish your goal(s)?

A philosophy of ministry is a stated reason why you do the things you do. A ministry is the act of serving God, His people, and the world. It stands to reason, then, that a philosophy of ministry is a stated reason why you serve God, His people, and the world. A philosophy of ministry is then a "controlling purpose," so to speak. It is my experience that most ministering people I know have not taken the time to think this through to the point that they can articulate their mission in life. Because of this short-circuit thought process, they often fall short of their goals, because they cannot state what it is or why they feel that way.

I am a strong believer in the emotional aspects of a call of God on an individual life. It seems to me that when the Lord speaks to us, He speaks to all of us. What I mean by that is the Lord is perfectly capable of making contact with all of me when He speaks: spirit, soul, and body. The subjective, experiential dimensions of a relationship with God are very important. But at some point, the experience – the sensation of it all – needs to give way to a well thought out and clearly expressed "mission statement." This keeps us on track if ever the memory of the initial experience wears thin.

In formulating a vision that is communicable to people, the leader must reinforce it with a reasonable philosophy based on the Word of God, and then implement it with a plan or a strategy that is "publishable" or clear and plain to the people following.

I maintain that the simpler it is the better. Embellishing Jesus' admonitions and commands is unnecessary. We will have all the work we will ever want just obeying His mandates without having to add anything else. It is this very characteristic of the Jerusalem church that attracted me first. They were too young in their way to have complicated or sophisticated their organization or message. We need to get back to this so that Jesus can shine through brighter to the outsider or the uninitiated.

Recently, I was sharing with a fellow pastor the plan I felt the Lord had given me for the next phase of our ministry. He interrupted me in the midst of my presentation with a question that startled me. "Jim, how can you get such a clear vision of what you are to do so that you can articulate it so confidently and clearly?" My answer, after a moment or two of hesitation, "Well, it never occurred to me that it would be any other way."

Over the years I have often been introduced to groups as "the man with a plan." Usually, they were referring to the written materials regarding our church's philosophy of ministry or church planting that I had written in order to prepare them for our future. I always thought the introduction curious because it never occurred to me that having a God-given plan and working it was a novel or unusual way of doing His work.

Back in the "Dark Ages," when I was attending L.I.F.E. Bible College in Los Angeles, California, one of my favorite professors was Dorothy Jean Furlong. I'll never fully realize the extent of the impact that one woman has had on my ministry, but I suspect the Lord is keeping track. I know that a simple quote I heard her share in an "Administration of Christian Education" course one morning in 1965 had a profound effect on my approach to the ministry. All she said was this, "People who fail to plan, plan to fail." At that particular time in Pentecostal circles there continued a debate as to whether planning ahead was unspiritual and contributed to the "quenching of the Holy Spirit." It seems that there were those who strongly felt that only the spontaneous carried with it the unction of the Spirit. Dr. Furlong was among those who dared to teach us that a plan that emitted from the heart of God was nothing to be ashamed of, and furthermore carried with it the potential of tremendously far-reaching consequences. So, I began then to pray, to think, to read, to talk, and then to plan.

TO PRAY
"In all your ways acknowledge Him, and He will make your paths straight."
—Proverbs 3:6

"Do not be anxious (or uncertain) about anything, but in everything, by prayer and petition with thanksgiving present your requests (questions) to God."
—Philippians 4:6

TO THINK
"Suppose one of you wants to build a tower. Will he not first sit down and estimate the cost to see if he has enough money to complete it?"
—Luke 14:28

TO READ
"Your word is a lamp to my feet and a light to my path."
[or my plan]
—Psalms 119:105

TO TALK
"Plans fail for lack of counsel, but with many advisers they succeed."

—Proverbs 15:22

TO PLAN
"Without a vision the people perish…"

—Proverbs 29:18

"Publish the vision and make it plain so they may run that read it."

—Habakkuk 2:2

I realize, of course, that this process is predicated on a fundamental assumption: that you have heard from God. We all know that kind of claim can be very presumptuous and at best subjective. So, the question that pastor asked me is valid. How can anyone know that they have heard from God and that their plan or vision is from His heart? (See Appendix VII "Have You Heard Any Voices Lately?")

FINALLY

I come to the end of this appeal with this final question: Is "A CHURCH WITHOUT WALLS" what you are looking for? If your dream is similar to mine, I encourage you to prayerfully seek the Lord about what is to be your response to the Scriptures and convictions found in these pages. It is never easy to "CONTEND FOR THE AUTHENTIC," but in the end it will be more than worth every effort! Let's get back to the basics!

APPENDIX I

REASONS WHY OUR CHURCH EXISTS

THE FOLLOWING IS in essence my philosophy of ministry for the local church. Each conviction is followed by phrases I have often used to speak to these issues in my preaching, teaching, and interaction in general with the congregation. At least one Scripture reference for each conviction is included, as is a concise list of rules that govern the implementation of the philosophical conviction into the strategy and program of the church.

A. **TO PREACH THE GOSPEL**, never compromising our community's basic need of a Savior. "Our highest priority is to see men, women, boys, and girls coming to know that they are right with God, and that their sins are forgiven through faith in Jesus Christ." (John 3:16)

1. Give public invitations for people to get saved regularly.
2. Train believers how to seize opportunities to share their faith.
3. Plan evangelistic events and send out evangelistic teams on a regular basis.
4. Develop a "Jerusalem, Judea, Samaria, and uttermost parts of the earth" strategy of ever-expanding concern for evangelism and mission.

B. **TO ESTABLISH A MINISTRY THAT AFFIRMS FAMILY**, not distracts from it. "We will not do for a family what God ordains a family to do for themselves." (Deut. 4:9, Proverbs 22:6)

1. Train parents to parent, take nothing for granted.
2. Provide minimal yet quality institutional education.
3. Keep the children involved in corporate worship.
4. Do not expect people to be away from home a lot.
5. Encourage and facilitate a "family night."
6. Carefully implement programming that integrates and unites the family.
7. Place the "solitary" in families.

C. **TO MAKE DISCIPLES, TEACHING THEM TO OBEY** the Scriptures and to find their individual expression of ministry. "Every member is a minister." "Anything healthy is reproducible." "Work yourself out of a job." "Teach people to do what you do, basically the same way you do it." (Matthew 28:19, 20; 2 Timothy 2:2)

1. Obedience-oriented preaching and teaching.
2. Emphasis is on a "non-clergy" approach to ministry.
3. Encourage every leader or worker to have a disciple.
4. Implement a small-group structure that releases ministry.
5. Do not start programs that cannot be reproduced.
6. Emphasis on the orderly delegation of authority, responsibility, and accountability.

D. **TO IDENTIFY THE HOME AS THE PRINCIPLE SITE OF MINISTRY.** "Home and church dynamics should be similar." "We obey the great commission from our front door." (Acts 2:46 and Acts 5:42)

1. Stress a clear definition of the church as people and not a place.
2. Encourage families to use their homes redemptively.
3. Instruct in the ministry of hospitality.
4. Prepare adults to disciple their own households.

E. **TO CONTEND FOR THE PRIORITY OF THE AUTHENTIC WORSHIP OF GOD.** "If we do nothing else, we will worship the Lord." "Worship is the atmosphere in which the Holy Spirit most freely works." (John 4:24, Psalm 111:1, Ephesians 5:19)

1. Worship will be the way we begin all of our meetings.
2. Worship will be taught and encouraged as a "way of life."

3. Do not allow music ministry to take place outside of a genuinely worshipful atmosphere, other than for evangelism.
4. We will not "worship" worship.
5. Model corporate worship in such a way that the participant sees it as something they could also do at home.
6. Teach children and youth how and why to worship.

F. **TO BE AS MUCH LIKE THE CHURCH OF THE BOOK OF ACTS AS POSSIBLE** in twenty-first century America. "Jesus is returning for a church like the one He left." "We must contend for the authentic." "New Testament churches are desperately needed today." (Acts 2:42-47, Eph. 5:27)

1. To follow the New Testament model of ministry very closely in all that we do.
2. The observance of Holy Communion will become the "highlight" of our monthly schedule.
3. Miracles, healings, and deliverance will be taught and encouraged as a normal and regular part of church life.
4. Emphasis will be placed on accountable church membership, baptism in water, and baptism in the Holy Spirit.

G. **TO BRING THE PEOPLE OF GOD INTO A "WORLD CHRISTIAN" CONTEXT** of life and ministry. "If we believe that Jesus could return in our lifetime, then that conviction has to have an effect upon the way we live our lives." "Each fellowship has its own 'Jerusalem, Judea, Samaria and uttermost parts of the earth.'" "No one has the right to hear the gospel twice until everyone has heard it once." (Matthew 24:14, 28:18-20, and John 17:23)

1. Stress the importance of unity with the rest of the Body of Christ – everywhere.
2. Encourage ministry to the poor and distressed.
3. Discourage needless accumulation of wealth and possessions.
4. Discourage waste, greed, and biases that betray an ethnocentrism view of the world.
5. Prepare workers to be sent out into the world as both "tent makers" and full-time missionaries.
6. Purpose to give a significant percentage of the church's income to the poor and to world evangelization.
7. Discover ways to regularly educate the congregation to the spiritual needs of other cultures.

H. **TO DISCOVER THE EFFECTIVENESS OF THE SMALLER GROUP** in maturing God's people and releasing their gifts. "Small groups should be the backbone of a body of believers." "We must have an organizational structure that facilitates the meeting of the individual's needs." "Small groups keep larger congregations from becoming impersonal." (Mark 3:7, 13, 14; Hebrews 10:19-25)

1. Train effective leaders to serve small groups.
2. Leaders must understand servanthood, authority submission, inductive Bible study, spiritual gifts, intercession, worship, and hospitality.
3. Develop curriculum for effective Bible study and discussion in small groups.

4. Allow some small groups to eventually become house churches that become indigenous churches.
5. Contend for a strong percentage of the congregation to be a part of some kind of small group.

I. **TO REPRODUCE THE LOCAL CHURCH AS OFTEN AS POSSIBLE** through church planting. "Anything that is healthy is reproducible." "We're going to have a baby!" "We need strong, healthy small and mid-size churches throughout the area, not just one big one." "We are a mother church that should be willing to constantly give ourselves away." (2 Corinthians 12:14)

1. Develop a way of adequately preparing and releasing leadership for new churches.
2. Make the vision for church planting clear so that it is "owned" by the entire congregation and they can rejoice when the time comes to give people away.
3. Cooperate with the denomination in church planting.
4. Look for opportunities to plant churches cross culturally.

J. **TO MAINTAIN AN INTERDENOMINATIONAL, NONSECTARIAN SPIRIT** in the community. "We are part of an interdenominational-denomination." "The Holy Spirit desires to bring the Body of Christ into unity, not uniformity." (Matthew 8:9, Ephesians 4:11, 5:21; Proverbs 24:6)

1. To promote unity and understanding among the various Christian congregations within our community.
2. Cooperate completely with the denomination, at all levels: Division, District, and International.
3. Be sure all new members understand the trans-local affiliations and responsibilities of our local church.
4. Support local and missionary endeavors on merit, regardless of denominational affiliations.

K. **TO DECLARE THAT THE KINGDOM OF GOD IS AT HAND.** "Let's not play church." "Every believer needs to know who he or she is IN Jesus Christ." "The gifts of the Spirit are for today." "The Kingdom of God is anywhere Jesus is recognized as Lord." (Hebrews 13:8; Mark 16:17-18; James 5:15)

1. Pray for the sick, anointing them with oil in the name of Jesus Christ.
2. Cast out demons.
3. Contend for the baptism of the Spirit as a spiritual experience that is not to be confused with salvation.
4. Teach every believer of the authority they have in Jesus Christ, and its holy application.

GOD HAS CALLED US TO:

• Walk in Worship - a people who understand their highest calling.
• Walk in Love - a people who genuinely care about one another.

- Walk in Mission - a people who compassionately give witness of their faith.
- Walk in Obedience - a people who honor God's Word by obeying it.
- Walk in Humility - a people who give God all the glory.
- Walk in Purity - a people who keep themselves from sin and all that opposes the knowledge of God.
- Walk in Simplicity—a people who keep it real, accessible, and uncomplicated.

APPENDIX II

SMALL GROUP LEADERS SHOULD:

1. Have a vital commitment to the local church body, walking in submission "one to another."

2. Be a willing student of the Word and disciplined in prayer.

3. Demonstrate and confess to spiritual growth and life in the Spirit.

4. Build strong, loving relationships within one's family and with others beyond the immediate family circle.

5. Have his/her home life in order – whether married or single.

6. Willingly practice hospitality.

7. Evidence ability to lead a small group around a common meal, discussion of spiritual matters, or lead a prayer time.

8. Be willing and ready to invest the necessary time for home group meetings, group prayer, fellowship, and training sessions.

9. Be willing to care for and bear the burden of ten to twenty other people.

10. Have a functional understanding and appreciation of spiritual gifts and ministry.

APPENDIX III

REASONS WHY THE CHURCH AND
THE HOME ARE INSEPARABLE

1. The very being of God was revealed through the creation of the human family. (Genesis 1:26-27)
2. The role of the church is biblically defined by the use of marriage and family terminology. (Ephesians 5:32; I Timothy 3:15)
3. Family qualifications are the standards required in Scripture for church leadership. (1 Timothy 3:2-4; 1 Thessalonians 2:11)
4. The first spiritual foundations of the church were laid in homes and family settings. (Mark 14:14; Acts 2:2, 46)
5. The church, in fact being the family of God, really only works as the church when it lives by family realities. (Matthew 23:6-8; 1 Timothy 5:1-2)

6. The physical family, in fact being the people of God, really works as a family when it lives by church realities. (1 Timothy 4:3-6; 1 Peter 3:7)
7. The Bible places full spiritual responsibility for training and discipline of children with parents, especially fathers, and not the institutional church. (Deuteronomy 6:5-7; Ephesians 6:4)

APPENDIX IV

WHY HAVE A HOME NIGHT?
(Dr. Don McGregor)

I. THREE THEOLOGICAL REASONS FOR HAVING A "HOME NIGHT"
   The phrase "Home Night" points to principles pertaining to Christianity as a way of life and to the church as the family of God. Once the theological assumptions are understood, such a thing as having a "Home Night" makes sense. At least three theological reasons support its significance:

   A. Family generations are central to the redemptive purposes of God. (Genesis 18:19; Isaiah 59:21) Both salvation and sanctification belong in a special way to home and family structures. (Acts 16:31; 1 Corinthians 7:14)

B. The main biblical call for Christian education takes place daily in homes and is done through the family's generation. (Psalm 78:5-7; Deuteronomy 6; Ephesians 6:4)

C. Christianity is a way of life, and the church functioning as the family of God is best lived out in natural settings in daily life. (Acts 2:42-47) Sadly, the church has been confused with physical, public buildings. Christianity often seems more like pulpits and classrooms rather than a redeemed people rescued from a crooked generation. (Acts 2:40) Christianity is not only verbal, it is vital! It must be experienced at the life level.

II. THREE PRACTICAL REASONS FOR HAVING A "HOME NIGHT"

A. "Home Night" visibly affirms the place and the priority of the home. "Home Night" obviously merges the medium and the message. Significant spiritual experiences at home and within families match the meaning of Christianity. It is helpful to note that the words "home" and "family" are not exactly the same thing. Singles are not left out by the word "home," for it represents the reality of our daily lives, regardless of how different that may be.

Even young people should be like Timothy and "set an example for all believers," treating the entire family of God exactly like they would their own parents, brothers, and sisters. (1 Timothy 4:11, 5:2) Here one should emulate the quality of Paul's personal relationships in Romans 16.

Hospitality is for everyone. It is not an "elective," open only for married couples and families with children. (Romans 12:13) Singles should share and lead in "Home Nights." In this way they can fulfill the claim of 1 Corinthians 7:32-35 and "promote good order." They are given the chance to serve "in the body and spirit" in ministry to families, who without exception will have "worldly troubles." (1 Corinthians 7:28) We should also note that when a husband or a father begins a "Home Night," with its visible affirmation of the priority of the home and family, he is meeting the number one need of every wife and mother, which is a stable, strong, spiritual leadership at home.

B. A "Home Night" establishes the power of good habits. The exhortation to "do all things decently and in order" has wide application. (1 Corinthians 14:40) Spiritual things do not take shape without some formality or form. A "Home Night" helps establish a regular and planned good habit. The writer to the Hebrews recognized the danger of letting things drift. (Hebrews 5:14) A regular "Home Night" allows our habits to work for us, and it becomes a weekly reminder of what we as Christian people are all about.

C. A "Home Night" makes possible the ministry purposes of our local congregation. A "Home Night" does more than serve an individual or a single family. It allows our homes to become centers of redemption to others. It makes us mutual at the place where it counts the most in our daily lives and in our homes. Spontaneous sharing of "Home Nights" allows for unlimited ministry with friends, neighbors, and all the family "clan." Nor should we overlook the need, literally, around the world. The witness of a body of believers with open homes and families in order is a testimony that could conceivably change the face of society. Certainly it would be a new "face for the church."

III. HOW TO HAVE A "HOME NIGHT"

    A. Do preliminary planning. Prayer and creative planning should precede a "Home Night." In fact, the first one could be spent with the entire household planning together. Periodically, these plans will need to be reviewed and revised. Fathers and husbands are essential to lead and approve in the family plans. Mothers with unsaved husbands should follow the counsel of 1 Peter 3:1-6 and manifest grace and wisdom before and with her children. Singles and single parents and their children should periodically or permanently join with others for "Home Night" as the Lord leads. A "Home Night" should be regarded as the most important meeting of the week, for it is here that the ministry of the priesthood of all believers is exercised and measured by real life.

    B. Establish a set time. Each household is different in size, age, and needs, so freedom and flexibility is expected. Whenever possible, establish a regular and set time for the gathering. Some congregations corporately designate a particular night of the week for cooperating families to have "Home Night." The church is careful not to violate that night with other programs or events.

    C. Adopt a formula that edifies your own household. By way of suggestion, many households have in various ways incorporated the following three general components:

1. Share a pleasant meal together. (Acts 2:46) A periodic shared meal with other families invited over for the evening adds to the joy.

2. Take time for personal and spiritual sharing. Include such things as singing, prayer, reading, and discussing passages of Scripture. Numerous resources are available. The pastor's sermon or Sunday school lessons can be shared and discussed. A review of the events of the past week and prayer for the coming week knit hearts together.

3. Have a fun time together with meaningful activities for everyone. Shared fun experiences are healing for children of all ages. (Proverbs 17:22)

IV. CONCLUSION: Start a "Home Night!"

APPENDIX V

THE BASIC INGREDIENTS OF DISCIPLESHIP

THE DISCIPLINE PROCESS as commanded by the Lord Jesus Christ (Matthew 28:18-19), defined and modeled by the apostle Paul (2 Timothy 2:2) as well as ever so many other Old and New Testament figures, includes a number of aspects.

The responsibility of the discipler is to recognize the grace of God in people's lives by observing evidence of anointing and testimony of calling. Once this is determined, the development of the individual for leadership can begin. The development includes: intellect, character, ministry skills, and good stewardship in general of relationships and abilities.

Jesus said, *"I will build my church, and the gates of hell will not prevail against it"* (Matthew 16:18). He has, however, chosen to work through people; thus the training of those He has chosen for leadership is of the highest priority.

The following is a straight-forward list of areas of spiritual and biblical understanding that need to serve as the basis of a discipleship curriculum for the potential as well as developing leader. These topics are foundational. Much can be added, but it seems to me that this "bare bones" curriculum must be presented in order to help a new leader be adequately and properly prepared for what lies ahead.

1. "How to Study the Bible - An Inductive Approach"

   The spiritual leader must be given the tools to grow personally and prepare diligently. This would include a general introduction to the Scriptures and specific instruction in how to study the Scriptures and how to use basic aids that are available.

2. "The Spiritual Life of a Leader"

   A leader must understand the dynamics of prayer, fasting, faith, obedience, and other types of spiritual discipline. All of this must be balanced with a perspective of the grace of God that protects the new leader from legalistic tendencies.

3. "The Kingdom of God"

   The Lordship of Jesus Christ, His rule and reign in the believer's life. Spiritual warfare, spiritual gifts, and signs and wonders all fit into this very important category of truth that releases the power of God.

4. "The Christian Family"

It is not to be compromised in any way. This important area must not be taken for granted. Parenting, marriage, and home life must be in order and biblically understood.

5. "The Church"

The nature of the church must be understood so that institutional tendencies are avoided as much as possible. Worship, ordinances, body life relationships, and organization of ministry come under this category.

6. "Leadership Development-Discipleship"

The leader must know how to reproduce himself. Recognizing, cultivating, and releasing ministry is a skill to be developed.

7. "Evangelism and Mission"

Challenge and equip for the propagation of the gospel through preaching, lifestyle, strategizing, and outreach efforts.

These areas of training can serve as a good foundation for a sound approach to training and disciplining leaders.

APPENDIX VI

A BIBLICAL PATTERN FOR CHURCH PLANTING

THE FOLLOWING IS a compilation of nine principles, scriptures, and personal convictions based on my own experiences as a "planter" pastor and from the experience gleaned from "mothering" a number of other congregations over the years. They have been compiled to serve as an orderly set of guidelines that could be used by any fellowship desiring to "reproduce" their kind by planting new churches in any country or culture.

The "Test of Truth" needs to be applied to these principles:

1. Does it agree with the Word of God?
2. Will it work at home?
3. Will it work all over the world?

The "Test of Conscious" also is applicable if the material "rings true" to the reader:

1. Is this part of your experience?
2. Do your children understand it?
3. What has to change in order to apply it?

As you read these principles, remember that anything worth doing is worth doing well, and the Bible says in John 8:32, *"Then you know the truth, and the truth will set you free."*

THE PRINCIPLE OF PREPARATION

"Do your best to present yourself to God as one approved, a workman who does not need to be ashamed and who correctly handles the Word of Truth."
—2 Timothy 2:15

There is no substitute for current information. Zeal and burden for the lost is undoubtedly from the Lord, but He has warned us that the blind cannot lead the blind unless they plan on spending time in a ditch. I believe that it is the responsibility of the church to adequately train men and women for the work of the ministry, patiently and carefully. I believe this is a process that is mostly personal in nature and only secondarily academic or institutional. There is nothing that can take the place of personal relationship between the teacher and the pupil.

The Principle of Preparation is predicated on the potential minister understanding clearly the claim and call of God on his or her life. There are only a few that are "chosen" for equipping eldership of the church (Ephesians 4:11), while all of God's people are called to some form of ministry or another. If one is in fact called of God for leadership ministry, then there will be incumbent in that life certain things that will confirm the call.

Gifts are not enough for effective ministry. There must be the attending grace of maturity in the Word and genuine Christian character. This is the goal of the preparation process: to bring men and women "into maturity" – balancing their gifts with character. The work of the local church, its elders, and deacons can then be summarized as:

> Bringing men and women into the image of Jesus Christ through recognizing, cultivating, and releasing their individual gifts. Never using people, always developing people!

THE PRINCIPLE OF DISCIPLESHIP

"And the things you have heard me say in the presence of many witnesses, entrust to reliable men who will also be qualified to teach others."
—1 Timothy 2:2

The personal development of ministry through the transfer of life principles on a one-to-one basis is what is called discipleship. Certainly we are not to do people's thinking and praying for them, but help them to be modeled and patterned into being able to think, pray, and act independently in a reliable manner. Ministry that possesses life flows out of real, live, personal relationships. "Follow me, as I follow Christ" is the scriptural exhortation we need.

The local pastor with a heart for church growth must understand that as he reproduces himself (gifts and calling) in other men and women, the church is bound to grow, multiply, and flourish. Therefore, a process or program of some kind must be established at the local church level to encourage the personal discipleship relationships between the elders of the church and those who feel called to be sent out to plant churches.

It is important to point out that the discipleship relationship does not cease to exist when the disciple is finally sent out to minister in his or her own right (see the Principle of Accountability). A relationship is not conditional upon the circumstances. Certainly, some roles within the relationship will change. However, the key to the future success of the disciple is to stay in relationship to his teacher. Disciplers begin by allowing the learner to watch them minister. This is followed by a time when the disciple carefully observes his disciple ministering. Then, it is time for each one to be free to repeat the process with someone else. The work of the local church, its elders, and deacons with respect to discipleship can be summarized as:

Teaching men and women how to minister the life of Jesus Christ is basically the same way you minister.

THE PRINCIPLE OF REPRODUCTION

"My dear children, for whom I am again the pains of childbirth until Christ is formed in you."
—Galatians 4:19

"From him the whole body, joined and held together by every supporting ligament, grows and builds itself up in love, as each part does its work."
—Ephesians 4:16

The New Testament Scriptures seem to be filled with analogies between the church and the human body. It is important that we make note of the intertwined dynamics of vibrant church life. We learn that each member of the Body of Christ has a unique and special role to play in the church and in God's grand scheme of things for the present age in which we live. Not only do individuals have a specific gift or function in God's plan, but I believe that each individual assembly of believers has a unique and distinct assignment in God's overall plan. It is our responsibility as Christians to discover our individual identity as well as our corporate identity so that we can actively take our place in what God is doing on the earth.

Healthy human bodies possess the joy and privilege of reproduction - the greatest single miracle in nature and the goal of almost every human heart. Each individual member of the Body of Christ has the privilege of reproducing himself or herself in much the same way through witness and faithfulness. Entire congregations should be committed to reproducing themselves in the form of new churches. Anything born of God that is viable and credible in the Holy Spirit should be able to reproduce itself. It seems to be a law of nature and principle of the Kingdom of God.

The work of the local church, its elders, and deacons with respect to spiritual reproduction can be summarized as:

> Anything that is born of the Holy Spirit is then responsible to the need and natural tendency of reproducing itself in similar form.

THE PRINCIPLE OF ELDERSHIP

"Do not be hasty in the laying on of hands."
—1 Timothy 5:22

"To the elders among you, I appeal as a fellow elder...be shepherd of God's flock that is under your care, serving as overseer not because you must, but because you are willing

as God wants you to be; not greedy for money, but eager to serve, not lording over those entrusted to you, but being examples to the flock."
—1 Peter 5:1-3

The whole purpose of planting a church is to reach out into a community and call people in Jesus' name to repentance and faith. It then becomes the joyous responsibility of the local leadership to bring these people into maturity. This cannot be accomplished by a novice in faith, no matter how talented or zealous he may be. *This is the work of an elder.* Going back to the previous Principle of Reproduction, we see that only an elder can reproduce an elder, and any healthy church is spiritually dependent upon receiving into their midst leadership that meets the criteria of 1 Timothy 3:1-7. Anything short of this is doomed to stunted growth or even death.

It is the work of the local church, its elders, and deacons with respect to the need for true elders to be sent forth as church planters to:

Remember that you cannot lead a person beyond the point that you have been yourself. God's people deserve sensitive, mature, seasoned leadership; certainly this is critical in the beginning stages of the church.

THE PRINCIPLE OF CONFIRMATION

"Trust in the Lord with all your heart and lean not on your own understanding; in all your ways acknowledge Him, and He will make your paths straight."
—Proverbs 3:5-6

"There is a way that seems right to a man, but the end of it is destruction."
—Proverbs 14:12

138

The best-laid plans of men fall miserably short of the necessary grace that is required from the throne of Jesus for a church planting to be successful and remain fruitful for years to come. We must know beyond any shadow of a doubt that God is in the plan, and that the confirmation of His will as He has promised us is present before we "stumble" into the place of our calling.

When this supernatural confirmation is received, there is unwavering faith, a spirit-filled boldness that possesses and keeps the heart and mind of the minister regardless of adversaries, disappointments or set backs. If this confirmation of God's presence and blessing on the effort is not received, the smallest complication can produce defeat, confusion, and disaster. The Lord desires from the outset to declare to His people: "This is the way, walk ye in it!" Like Abraham, we must be able to point to an "altar" and say with settled peace, "That is where God spoke to me, giving me the promise."

You see, the truth is that there is a right person for the right place at the right time. Only our Alpha and Omega from His incredible vantage point understands all of those components and when to blend them together into a mighty move of His Spirit in a place. It is imperative that the prospective "pioneer" pastor have authoritative confirmation of all three of these conditions. We must remember:

> Without a supernatural revelation of the place, the strategy and an inner peace that God has ordained it to be, defeat and doubt will come quickly.

THE PRINCIPLE OF TWO BY TWO

"Calling the twelve to Himself, Jesus sent them out two by two and gave them authority over evil spirits...they went out and preached that people should repent..."
—Mark 6:7-12

The above passage of Scripture gives several important clues to the attitude and behavior of a "sent one." The serious student of church planting should study carefully this passage for personal revelation. The principle of sending out workers in groups (two by two) speaks of the complimentary grace of a team ministry that brings to the new fellowship an array of gifts and ministries that will bring the new congregation into its potential in an expeditious and balanced process.

I personally feel that the team approach is a point of spiritual and ministerial excellence that points out the equal value of deacons and elders in the church. It emphasizes the need to understand temperaments, personalities, spiritual gifts callings, and offices in the church. All of these things must be learned by the team before the work can properly begin.

The team of ministers should recognize that there can only be one leader. The presiding elder will undoubtedly be the spokesman, the principle teacher and spiritual leader of the team and the congregation that will be assembled together. The team should never become a spiritual club, power group, or clique – simply a group of servants called to the particular city, wanting to help according to their gifts and offices. I feel that the ideal team would include at least one elder and one deacon.

These teams cannot be "forced." It is a work of the Holy Spirit that sovereignly melds people's hearts together and gives them a common vision and a desire to serve one another and God's people. The potential pioneer should pray much about this and not make the mistake of inviting his friends to come along for the ride, but wait upon God of that complimentary ministry that will "round him out" in his ministry.

Jesus sent His disciples forth by pairs so that together they could face anything, comfort one another, and compliment the gifts and ministries Jesus gives each one.

THE PRINCIPLE OF PARENTHOOD

"After all, children should not have to save up for their parents, but for their children...I have not been a burden to you."
—2 Corinthians 12:14

It is important that pioneer workers not be a liability to the community and young church that they have come to serve. In every way they must be a very positive asset. We must remember that the biblical pattern is for "the elder to serve the younger," and "we do not come to be served... but to serve." This, of course, applies to every area of life: financial, emotional, spiritual, intellectual, and relational.

Many church planting efforts fail before they are hardly started because of the immediate emphasis upon supporting the pastor, building a building, or getting involved in other fund-raising projects before the proper foundation of relationships and biblical teaching on commitment have been able to happen. In my opinion, one of the most important services the mother congregation can contribute to the "baby church" is relief in this area. Support of the pioneer pastor and his family and other major expenses, such as rent on a meeting place, can be taken off their shoulders through the missionary giving of the sponsoring church. This support is then evaluated and adjusted by a graduating scale determined by the ability of the new church to accept its responsibility over the first three to twelve months of operation.

A young church will find its proper place in a new community much better if there is no need to begin immediately appealing for funds.

THE PRINCIPLE OF NON-CONVENIENCE

"The body of Christ is a unit, though it is made up of many parts: and though all its parts are many, they form one body."
—1 Corinthians 12:12

The birth of a new congregation as the extension of an existing congregation is an exciting yet traumatic event. Like birth itself, there is both joy and pain. The joy always wins out over the pain, yet both dynamics are a reality. A healthy birth is wholly dependent upon a healthy mother and a skilled deliverer. Jesus is the one who has promised to make the delivery. Now the question is: "Is the mother ready and healthy?"

A careful, analytical study of passages of Scripture like 1 Corinthians 12:12-27 is important at a time like this. Every member of the congregation sponsoring this "live birth" needs to understand the principles of body life.

The Principle of Non-convenience stems from the fact that many people within the sponsoring congregation are going to be placed in the inevitable position of having to make a choice – a choice regarding whether it is the Lord's will for them to be a part of the new body or to stay with the mother church. If this decision is not reached in a truly

Spirit-led way, they will only create problems for themselves and, consequently, both congregations.

The pastor of the sponsoring congregation will need to carefully lead the people God has entrusted to him into this decision-making process with strict accountability to the Word of God. The decision arrived at by the various members must be based on an inner witness of the Spirit, confirmed by the eldership that their gifts and ministries are needed in forming the nucleus of the new congregation. Their decision must never be based on mere convenience or reasons of taste. The Scriptures teach us that Jesus is the one with the architectural plan that He has prepared before the foundations of time. (Romans 12) When the Lord places someone in membership in a particular body of believers, one must be sure to answer the question: Has God changed His mind about where I belong?

When a congregation births another congregation, human reasoning has little to do with which families are to join the new congregation from the old. It is based on an understanding of God's will and plan, not mere convenience.

I would go so far as to say that if a congregation is starting a new church simply for the reason of convenience for a group of its people who live some distance from the meeting place, they fail to have sufficient reason for doing so. The planting of churches is only justified when a congregation is moved upon by the Holy Spirit to respond to the Great Commission of Jesus Christ. The purpose of new churches is to evangelize and disciple untouched communities, not to start a "convenience clique."

THE PRINCIPLE OF ACCOUNTABILITY

"Let the younger, in the same way be submissive to the older.
Clothe yourself with humanity toward one another."
—1 Peter 5:5

During the early stages of the new church's emergence into a community, it is wise that they remain under the protective and supportive covering of the sponsoring (mother) congregation. It is incumbent within the responsibility of the mother church to teach its child how to take care of itself. Just as a human mother will teach her child to feed itself and learn how to walk, I believe this process is natural to the birthing and training of a young church.

How this is exactly, practically worked out is crucial. It is at this point that many sponsoring congregations fail. We must not toss our babies out into a hostile environment without:

1. **Systematic intercessory support** before, during, and after the new church is birthed.
2. **Access to the new congregation for teaching and preaching** to augment the new pastor and confirm his word.
3. **Financial subsidy** until the new church can stand on its own feet.
4. **Regular and clear communication** between the sponsoring pastor and the young pastor.
5. **Cooperative activities** between the two congregations as often as is practical and within logistical possibilities.
6. **Administrative assistance and financial accountability** until the new church is self-supporting.

Because our church-planting strategy operates within the confines and relationship of our denominational affiliation, it is of vital importance that the new congregation develops a close relationship with the district supervisor. His counsel, support, and prayers will become a vital link to the denomination's other churches in the general area. The new church will be taught to cooperate in every way with the denominational strategy and program, becoming a viable part of Christ's body.

Credentials, licenses, insurances, and tax matters must all be channeled through the supervisor's office and staff. When the time comes for the new church to be chartered with the denomination, the time has probably come for the financial and legal aspects of the above-outlined relationship with the mother church to be discontinued. From that time on, these kinds of things will most likely be taken care of by the new church's leadership in direct communication with the district.

It is important that there be at all times a climate of trust and clear communication between the district supervisor, sponsoring pastor, and the new pastor. A new church is like a baby that needs to stand, toddle, walk, and then run. This growth responsibility is shared with the new church by the sponsoring church and other powers that be. Communication and accountability in a climate of trust is necessary for the success of the new church.

APPENDIX VII

HAVE YOU HEARD ANY VOICES LATELY?

What is a call? (An invitation to participate in God's redemptive plan)

"The one who calls you is faithful and he will do it."
—1 Thessalonians 5:24

"Trust in the Lord with all your heart and lean not on your own understanding; in all your ways acknowledge him, and he will make your paths straight."
—Proverbs 3:5-6

"The watchman opens the gate for him, and the sheep listen to his voice. He calls his own sheep by name and leads them out. When he has brought out all his own, he goes on ahead of them, and his sheep follow him because they know his voice."
—John 10:3-4

SIX PRINCIPLES AND SIX QUESTIONS TO HELP UNDERSTAND GOD'S WILL

1. **Principle of Volition** (Jeremiah 2:24)
    If you insist upon your way, you will get it. However, you must be prepared to experience the consequences.
    When...will I finally die to self interests?

2. **Principle of Revelation** (Genesis 12:7 & 13:4)
    For a calling to endure under all circumstances, it is imperative that one has undoubtedly heard from God distinctly and undeniably.
    Where...was I when the Lord showed me who I was and what I am to do?

3. **Principle of Confirmation** (Proverbs 20:18)
    The Lord has instituted an authority structure within the body as well as unmistakable perimeters witnessed by the Holy Spirit to establish His will.
    How...have I attempted to be sure my plans are valid?

4. **Principle of Qualification** (John 15:8)
    God does not call us to failure. He uniquely prepares each one of us for fruitfulness.
    Who...am I? Am I suited and gifted to accomplish the task?

5. **Principle of Justification** (Romans 12:6 and I Corinthians 12:4-6)
    There is always a very good and very distinctive reason why God tells people to do something.
    What...exactly do I have to offer that will extend the kingdom of God where I have been called?

ABOUT THE AUTHOR

JIM HAYFORD AND his wife, Betsey, have served as senior pastors in the Foursquare Church for forty-five years. Their three children, all grown, live in various parts of the state of Washington. The church they planted in northern California referred to in this book is now pastored by Cliff and Mari Hanes and was renamed several years ago to Eastbay Fellowship. The church continues to prosper. The Hayfords welcome response to the ideas presented in this book. Jim is available as a preacher, teacher, lecturer, and consultant. They can be reached by writing:

Eastside Foursquare Church
PO Box 1439
Bothell, WA 98041

CPSIA information can be obtained at www.ICGtesting.com
264457BV00001B/28/P